Pastor Bob's
VALLEY OF DEPRESSION, MOUNTAIN OF VICTORY

By

Rev. Robert E. Stoudt

PRESS

ACKNOWLEDGMENTS

First and foremost, I would like to acknowledge and give thanks to my Savior and Lord, Jesus Christ. He has allowed me to go through a deep trial. He was with me every step of the way. In fact, He is always with us and never leaves us. I give Him glory, honor and praise.

Secondly, I would like to acknowledge my wife, Frederica, of 46 years. As a caregiver, she sacrificed much during these past ten years. To this day she protects and keeps me from going backwards. She has much insight to give because she went through the process with me. She put a lot of time into editing this book. I love her, giving thanks for her great love for Jesus and for me.

Thirdly, I would like to acknowledge my children and grandchildren. I thank them for being patient and loving me during this time of my depression. I love them very much.

Fourthly, I would like to acknowledge the many friends that came alongside and encouraged me. Sharing of their own experiences of depression was a comfort to me. They prayed for me and with me.

Finally, I would like to acknowledge three friends who were a Godsend; Barbara Fulforth, Jack Ham, and Rona Lee. They came into my life in God's timing. I want to thank them for editing this book and the good advice they offered. Also, I thank Rona Lee for typing this manuscript. All of them truly have a heart for God, what a blessing.

PREFACE

This is a true account of Rev. Robert E. Stoudt, better known by his parishioners as Pastor Bob, who went from mountain top experiences to the long, lonesome valley of deep, dark depression and back again. This true account proves that no matter how hard a circumstance is, it is possible to overcome with the Lord's help. The author wants this account of his depression to be of help to those who are going through this deep valley. Rev. Robert E. Stoudt has been a pastor for forty-two years in seven different locations.

TABLE OF CONTENTS

FOREWORD

Following are some purposes why I wrote this book. As you read through the book, you will find various places of repetition; this is intentional. This book is written in topical form, not always chronological. For the most part it covers the spring and summer of 2001.

The <u>first</u> purpose for writing this book is to be of help to those who are going through the deep, dark valley of depression. I want to be as transparent and intimate about my journey as possible. If I'm not honestly open with the individual going through depression, then I'm only helping that individual to a certain level, but I did hit bottom in my depression. I have taken that journey to the point of coming short of death. You are not alone. I know through experience, not just knowledge, where you are. The struggles that I had, you may also have: the struggles of your mind, your thoughts — the thought of "hopelessness" and the thought of "I don't think I can get through this," the thought of "Will this ever end?", and the thought of "Is there anyone who will understand my struggles?". The answer is Yes! God always knows and when you connect with another person who has or is going through depression, they know also. This becomes one of the healing factors to an individual. The progress is different for each person. My recovery was very, very slow. The reason: I did not remove myself from the situation that caused my depression. My advice is to get professional help as soon as possible!

The <u>second</u> purpose for writing this book is to challenge each one of you to set in your minds that you *will* get through this, saying to yourself, "I will triumph," "I can do this, yes I can!" I found a Bible passage that says, *"Now thanks be to God, which always causes us to triumph in Christ..."* (II Corinthians 2:14a). You will have to push yourself hard, remove yourself as much as possible from the stressful and depressing situation. It's not easy; it takes work, lots of work. The mind has to be determined, no matter how you feel. You might have to live one minute at a time, one second at a time, and literally take one step at a time. The time will come, however, when you can live a fairly normal life again with some limitations. Dealing with the mind was the hardest thing I have ever done.

The <u>third</u> purpose for writing this book is to show and inform you that depression is no respecter of persons. People from every walk of life experience it: the rich, the poor, the famous and even the not-so-famous. From the greatest leadership positions that one could have to the lowest servitude responsibilities, depression shows no partiality — people such as factory workers, doctors, family members, movie stars, sports figures, housewives, farmers, preachers, retired individuals, bus drivers, school teachers, businessmen and the list could go on and on.

The <u>fourth</u> purpose for writing this book is to make you aware of the fact that you will have limitations after you have recovered from the stress and depression. Be aware, as much as possible, of what causes your depression. Take care of yourself, learn to say no and don't worry about what others think. If a person breaks a leg or has surgery of some sort that can be seen, people accept the injury and recovery time. On the other hand, what is occurring in the mind is very hard for others to accept, as your condition isn't visible and some become very critical. In my case as pastor of forty-two years in seven different churches, I had to resign my position nine years after the depression. After speaking for thirty minutes I was completely exhausted. Recently, I spoke in a church after being absent from the pulpit for thirteen months. I had to prepare for that message by studying and getting lots of sleep the night before. After speaking, I required lots of sleep and rest. In Chapter 11, I list some things that affected my depression along with what helped me. My vocation in life has changed.

The fifth purpose for writing this book has to do with one's relatives and friends gaining a knowledge of what you are going through without experiencing it themselves. They can only sympathize and understand to a limited degree. People need to understand what they cannot see or feel. This is the hardest time for both the depressed person and the caregiver. My wife, day after day, was perplexed, as I could tell by her countenance. Also, friends and family were at a loss of how to act or what to do. The greatest thing that a caregiver can do is give all the support possible to the one experiencing depression. My spouse, children, grandchildren, church family and friends gave me unconditional support.

You will find great comfort when you connect with a person who is or has gone through the same experience as you. I met six people who were and had experienced the depression that I was going through. I connected with a pastor who attended our church during the summers and he had great insight into what I was going through even though he did not go through the trauma himself. He prayed with me and had genuine sympathy. To people who do not understand what you are going through, your outward appearance looks healthy but in your mind you are suffering. Mental health facilities have pamphlets that will help both parties.

The <u>sixth</u> purpose for writing this book is to show you there is hope and deliverance. Because I am a pastor and because I know Jesus as my personal Savior, I will at times share what I believe from the Bible. I am not trying to convert you to know Jesus in a personal way, but I do want to help you through your own personal valley of deep, dark depression. If you were to share your experiences of depression, you would probably illustrate from your profession as I will be doing in this book. I do love seeing folks receive Jesus as their Savior and have the assurance that Heaven is their home. Chapter 13 explains how you can receive Jesus as Savior; that decision is completely up to you. I have prepared, through writing this book, a help through the deep, dark valley of depression.

CHAPTER 1

DESCENT INTO THE DEEP, DARK VALLEY OF DEPRESSION

God On The Mountain

Life is easy when you're up on the mountain

And you've got peace of mind like you've never known.

But then things change and you're down in the valley.

Don't lose faith for you're never alone.

For the God on the mountain is still God in the valley,

When things go wrong, He'll make it right.

And the God of the good times

is still God in the bad times.

The God of the day is still God in the night.

You talk of faith when you're up on the mountain.

Oh but the talk comes easy when life's at its best.

But it's down in the valley of trials and temptation

That's when faith is really put to the test.

For the God on the mountain is still God in the valley.

When things go wrong, He'll make it right.

And the God of the good times

is still God in the bad times.

The God of the day is still God in the night.

by Lynda Randle

As I begin this chapter, I want to reveal to you why I went through the deep, dark valley of depression. It was the result of several funerals, four of them critical, that happened in a three-week period of time. At the end of this chapter I have listed reasons that others have personally shared with me of why they entered their journey of depression.

In the spring of 2000, the harsh winter had passed and spring was well underway. The snowbirds were returning from their time in the South to upstate New York. News came to us about our daughter's father-in-law having lung cancer as they returned from Florida. Up to this point our beliefs were different and we would spend time together talking about various things. Now I spent the summer vis-

iting him and his wife every Thursday. I would read a portion of the Bible and pray with them, knowing that God's
Word, the Bible, gives comfort. When things hit rock bottom
in our lives, there is only one way to look, and that is, up. We
cry out to God and see His healing. As time passed, this man
got worse and in October 2000 he passed away.

It's interesting that I would meet with him every Thursday
through that summer and then he dies on a Thursday. On
the Tuesday before his passing, the Lord laid it on my heart
that morning to travel an hour to the hospital and speak with
him about his eternal destination. When I entered his room
no one else was around. I took a pamphlet from my pocket
which had Bible verses on it that explained how to get to
Heaven. I showed him how Jesus could take him to Heaven.
That morning he gave his heart and life to Jesus. For the
remaining two days of his life he took that pamphlet and
showed it to everyone who came into his room. What a witness for a brief two days! On that Thursday he went into the
presence of Jesus.

In the same month a deacon from my former church in the
foothills of the Adirondack Mountains in upstate New York
died and I conducted his memorial service at the cemetery.
It was a beautiful autumn day. The following month, being

November, my niece's father-in-law was on his deathbed. We had gone to my daughter's home on Thanksgiving eve to take a few days off for the holiday. I received a call to visit him and his family in their home. That night as I shared with him about Jesus, he recommitted his life to the Lord. Soon after he passed away. I believe that I conducted his funeral, although I do not clearly remember it.

After going through the holiday season, things were settling down as we began the new year of 2001. We heard again of one of our townspeople who had liver cancer and did not have much time to live. In my time as pastor there, I cannot remember a time that he was in our church but I was friends with him. At his passing I was approached by the family and asked if I would conduct the funeral service and I said yes. It was a small town and he was well known in the community and surrounding towns. There were over three hundred people in attendance at his funeral. The former pastor and his wife were members of our church and also worked with him and others in the community when they were teenagers. The former pastor was asked to give the eulogy and he shared how this man as a teenager asked Jesus to come into his life.

This was the fourth funeral I had conducted in four months, and two that really had an impact on me, our church people and the community in which we lived. This man was only forty-four years of age. As my wife and her friend walked across the parking lot to attend his funeral service, the friend turned to my wife and said, "He is so young." Soon after the funeral, my wife and I took a trip to Ohio where my father and sisters live. We were exhausted from spending time counseling the family and conducting the funerals. We welcomed a much needed rest. Just as a passing note, a pastor and his wife are human, like everyone else and we need rest and a time to recharge like everyone else does.

At this same time my daughter, her husband and children, were living with us during the time of this funeral and the ones to follow. They had just moved back from South Carolina, as they needed a place to stay for three or four weeks until their house was available to move into.

When we returned from our trip, we received a phone call from my wife's friend's husband who was also a deacon in our church. His wife had gone in for an outpatient operation and the husband said, "It doesn't look good." My wife asked, "What doesn't look good?" He just kept saying, "It just doesn't look good." This is the same person who said to my wife two weeks earlier at the funeral, "He is so young." Now *she* was in critical condition in the hospital. We quickly drove the hour to the hospital and met her husband there. He told us she was put on life support. This woman remained hooked to life support for four days. During that time, friends and neighbors were at the hospital showing their support to the family. There were between twenty-five and thirty people there the four days she was in the hospital. All day and into the evening I and the deacons, along with my wife, were in the hospital doing counseling. I remember clearly walking to the water fountain on the fourth day and the Spirit of God said to my mind, "You are going too far," and I did. My wife could not come with me there that day and I should have stayed home as well. On the fourth day, the life support system was turned off and my wife's friend was pronounced dead. She knew Jesus as her Savior and at that time entered into Heaven. She was thirty-seven and left behind a husband and a six-year-old daughter. There were 275 people present at her funeral. I had two funeral services for her, one in our town and the other in her hometown about 100 miles away.

Two weeks later my wife's brother, who was fifty-seven, retired two years before and lived in Ohio, had a massive heart attack as he was driving and died before he could get his vehicle off the road. A miracle took place. The van he was driving went up an embankment, between two trees that you and I would have a hard time driving through and bumped up against a garage. I believe it was driven by angels. He too, knew the Lord and went into His presence.

Again, I mention these things because they were the cause of my going into depression. I just overextended myself. After returning home from his funeral, things started to settle down. I didn't realize I was in such bad shape.

There were other things that happened to people that we knew. For example, my other daughter's brother-in-law dove into the water, hit a rock and broke his neck and my wife felt she could not share this with me as she knew how stressed and spent I was. From this time on in 2001 I tried to be out and about but it was difficult. I tried to go to places I liked, for example, the fair. When I would see people with gray and white hair, it bothered me considerably because it reminded me of death. Seeing a dead animal on or next to the road would stir up feelings of death. To go into a funeral parlor was so stressful. I was not able to perform funerals for a while but eventually I did conduct funerals up to the time of my retirement as pastor in 2010. To this day I only go into funeral homes for a brief time.

As I mentioned at the beginning of this chapter, the following are some reasons why people descend into the deep, dark valley of depression and despair as told to me:

1. Some businesspeople, having had a huge loss in their business, are sent into depression and despair.

2. Parents whose children develop "wings" and "fly out of the nest" can become depressed and go into despair because of the big changes in the life of their family.

3. Couples and families who have pulled up roots and moved to a new location because of employment can experience despair and depression because they feel alone and deserted.

4. New mothers, after giving birth, may experience post-partum depression.

5. People about whom lies are told may lose everything and go into depression.

6. I learned of a woman who was dealing with a husband with an addiction. She found this very difficult to deal with and when she saw a fire and the suddenness of a word or action, she would go into a depression.

7. Another example is of a businessman who had an only child, a son graduating from high school. Realizing how this would affect their family dynamics, the father went into a deep, dark depression.

8. In my own case, because of so many funerals occurring in such a short period of time, I depleted the use of serotonin in my brain and it put me into depression and despair. Every time I saw a person who had gray hair, it was like I was seeing death written across their forehead.

Encouragement from the Bible, God's Word

"Many are the afflictions of the righteous, But the LORD delivers him out of them all." (Psalm 34:19)

"Trust in the LORD, and do good; Dwell in the land, and feed on His faithfulness. Delight yourself also in the LORD, and He shall give you the desires of your heart. Commit your way to the LORD. Trust also in Him, ... Rest in the LORD, and wait patiently for Him..." (Psalm 37: 3,5,7)

CHAPTER 2

SHADOW OF DEATH

Head Trauma #1, Harrisburg, Pennsylvania

I had been taken to the hospital by ambulance from a meeting I was attending. The next day I had a stress test, then was released from the hospital. My wife and I headed home, packed our clothes and headed for North Carolina for vacation. We stopped at Wilkes-Barre, Pennsylvania for the night. The next morning I woke up anxious, but okay. The day consisted of low, fast-moving clouds with light drizzle. We stopped at a McDonald's for breakfast in Frackville, Pennsylvania. Everything was fine. Going through the mountains, the elevation changed quite often. The further we traveled, the change in elevation caused head trauma and disorientation to me. As we arrived at Harrisburg, Pennsylvania we decided to stop for a break. I pulled our vehicle into a

McDonald's parking lot and that's where big changes and a turn for the worse took place in my health. I stepped out of my vehicle and the pressure in my head was so great, my head felt twice its size. As I walked toward the restaurant I thought to myself, this is it. I was expecting to drop dead right there on the spot. With the good Lord's grace and mercy, I made it through. We left McDonald's and drove a little further south. The trauma just got worse. I said to my wife, I need to turn around and head for home". I needed help.

Up to this point I was driving, but I was so bad that my wife had to do the driving. As we headed home, along with the head trauma, panic attacks started. As the day passed, the head trauma, severe stress, panic attacks and depression set in. I was in pretty bad shape by the time we arrived home.

The next day we drove six hours to my sister-in-law's place. I was going to try recovery through the natural way: herbs. I went to an herbalist, a person trained in recommending various herbs for wellness. I can tell you that because of the severity of my condition, as the days passed, this type of therapy did not work. I am not opposed to the natural use of herbs, but my condition was too severe at the time. The two days we were at her home, I found relief for a few minutes by engaging in some physical work, but it did not last. Folks who have depression, head trauma and stress, value every minute of relief they get. I even tried a massage and relaxation to soft music. I panicked and could not do it.

The trip out and back was excruciating, constantly in panic mode and head trauma. We arrived home and I continued trying to use herbs for my recovery, but once again, that did not work. I had a friend who used them for eight years and never felt complete until he got on medicine.

As the summer passed, I can now recall one day when my wife had gone out and I was on the back porch alone and secluded from people. It was a sunny, warm day. I took a chair and placed it in the sun and laid back and rested peaceably for two hours. Oh! What a relief it was from my head trauma. To this day I love to feel the warmth of the sun on my head and the sunshiny days. It really makes my head feel good. The Lord was gracious to allow us to move to Florida in 2011.

Head Trauma #2, My Bedroom

We were living in the Adirondack Mountains of upstate New York. One night as I continued my descent to the deep, dark valley of depression, I got up about 2:00 a.m. in the morning to go to the bathroom. As soon as I stood up, the back of my head hurt with excruciating pain, to the point that I thought, for the second time, that I would drop dead on the spot. The area was the size of a silver dollar and the pain lasted about five minutes. It felt like, what some have described as an aneurism. Again I was surprised I was still alive.

I talked to a doctor friend of mine and he said any one of the head traumas could have been fatal. God spared my life again, He is so good to me, Praise His Holy Name!!

Head Trauma #3, The River

I'm sitting at the small picnic grounds by the river where, I faced another head trauma. I'm looking up at the picnic table nestled in the trees, on a huge rock, overlooking a large waterfall. I had spent several days at that spot crying out to God for His help and mercy. Again, as I sat at that picnic table, my head hurt so badly I could feel at any moment my life would be taken from me. As at other times, stress and depression were prevalent. My head felt disoriented and my eyes could not focus well.

You might say, "Pastor Bob, it sounds like you were crazy." I would not argue with you one bit. It was not that I was crazy, but there was a clinical issue. There was a chemical imbalance in my brain. Today, as I sit here, everything is normal and my brain is functioning well. The Bible says, in I Thessalonians 5:23b: *"... may your whole spirit, soul and body be preserved blameless at the coming of our Lord Jesus Christ."* Man is a three-part being spirit, soul and body – and I learned through counseling that if you get any one of these out of kilter, the other two are affected. Because I overextended myself by helping people, I developed a chemical imbalance in my brain; as a result I lost weight and was in a spiritual warfare.

Head Trauma #4, Back Porch

As I stood on the back porch day after day, trying to hold in check the trauma in my head, the sensations in my head gave me the feeling that I did not know if I was going to live or die. It is hard to explain but let me try. Say you have a decision to make between two things. You cannot choose what decision to make. You might use the phrase, "this thing is driving me crazy."

It was similar to when, after I graduated from Bible school, I thought I had to immediately go some place to serve, but the Lord was teaching me to wait until He was ready. I said to my wife that this trying to decide is really driving me crazy. I just banged my head against the wall, but that did not really help. Six months later the Lord gave me a place to serve.

I tried to explain my feelings to my wife, but she could not comprehend what I was talking about. It was like I was stuck in neutral. One moment I would shift into the feeling I was going to live, the next moment I felt as if I were going to die. This was the terrible, excruciating feeling that I experienced for several days. Wow! What a ride.

Because of the head trauma, it drove me to memorize Bible verses. I memorized some two hundred verses in the four months of my deepest depression in 2001. I would put the verses on 3x5 cards and memorize them as I walked. For some reason I could not watch television, eat or sleep in the house. I could not listen to tapes, CDs, sermons or music that had words or an upbeat to them. I could walk and listen to soft, soothing music on a portable CD player. I carried a CD player with me everywhere I went. The Bible, in I Samuel 16:14, says: *"...the [Holy] Spirit of the Lord departed from Saul, and a distressing spirit from the LORD troubled him."* Some say the distressing spirit was God causing Saul to have spells in which he felt miserable, perhaps even periods of severe depression. In I Samuel 16:23 the Bible says, *"And so it was, whenever the spirit from God was upon Saul, that David would take his harp [soft music] and play it with his hand. Then Saul would become refreshed and well, and the distressing spirit would depart from him."* Bottom line, find something you enjoy and focus on it.

Head Trauma #5, My Daughter's Place

My wife and I would go back and forth from the church where I pastored to my daughter's place forty miles away. This particular day, it was very dreary and drizzly and the clouds were low and fast moving. This kind of weather would take a big toll on my head. Again, it felt like I did not know if I were going to live or die. My wife drove me down the road a little ways, stopped the car and I got out. She tried to calm me down, but it didn't work. I pranced around the car holding my head, feeling like it was going to explode. That lasted for two days, then the weather changed. Again, it is something very hard to relate to those who have never gone through it. While at my daughter's place I would try to do some projects but I could only do them for a short time and then my brain could not handle the head strain.

Head Trauma #6, Car Garage

Another time I thought I was going to succumb to death was while I was eating my supper at the entrance to the garage. It was shortly before 5:00 p.m. when my wife brought supper to me. This took place during the six weeks I could not eat or sleep inside. I said to her, "I just can't handle this anymore. I just can't! I don't know what I'm going to do." My wife then called the doctor and described my condition to him. He then talked to me on the phone. After a couple of minutes he told me to give the phone back to my wife, as I wasn't able to comprehend what needs to be said and done. When my wife got back on the phone, the doctor said to her, "I didn't realize that Bob was so bad." He was just leaving the office but said he would write a prescription and drop it off at the pharmacy. I was so distraught that my wife did not want to leave me alone, so she called a deacon from our church to come over and stay with me while she went to pick up the medicine. She arrived home about an hour later and I took the medicine. I began to relax and that night and the nights to follow I was able to sleep and eat inside the house. What a blessing from the Lord.

Knowing Jesus as my Savior and Shepherd, I know that He will guide me to the other side of the valley. In the past we have traveled I-75 from Ohio into West Virginia. There are two places that travelers pass, not over the mountain, but through it. As you approach those areas there are signs that say, "Turn your headlights on." As you get closer to the tunnel, all you see is a black hole. Yes, there are lights inside but it is much darker than the daylight outside. After you travel a ways through the tunnel, you see the light at that end. Like that tunnel, we go through hard times, dark times of depression, but Jesus will guide us through. We get encouragement from a very familiar passage in God's Word:

*"The LORD is __my__ shepherd; I shall not want [lack]. He makes me to lie down in green pastures; He leads me beside the still waters. He restores my soul; He leads me in the paths of righteousness for His name's sake. Yea, though **I walk through the valley of the shadow of death**, I will fear no evil. **For You are with me**. Your rod and staff, they comfort me. You prepare a table before me in the presence of my enemies; You anoint my head with oil; My cup runs over. Surely goodness and mercy shall follow me all the days of my life; and I will dwell in the house of the LORD forever."* (Psalm 23)

The lyrics to Josh Groban's song, "You Raise Me Up," speak to this so eloquently as well:

> When I am down and, oh my soul, so weary;
> When troubles come and my heart burdened be;
> Then, I am still and wait here in the silence,
> Until you come and sit awhile with me.

> There is no life – no life without its hunger;
> Each restless heart beats so imperfectly;
> But when you come and I am filled with wonder,
> Sometimes, I think I glimpse eternity.

> You raise me up, so I can stand on mountains;
> You raise me up, to walk on stormy seas;
> I am strong, when I am on your shoulders;
> You raise me up ... To more than I can be.
> You raise me up ... To more than I can be.

CHAPTER 3

EXTREME PANIC ATTACKS

O h no, I can't swallow. What do I do? I don't know if I can stand it. While walking through the tunnel to a conference center in Rochester, New York, I got such a hard panic attack, I could not even swallow. We were there to see the Gaithers concert. It lasted four hours plus. During that time, one panic attack followed another. It was no easier leaving the building than was coming in. As I journeyed through that tunnel, I found I could not swallow because of the panic attacks.

Pastor Bob midway through his depression

In the previous chapter I mentioned that leaving Harrisburg Pennsylvania we turned around and headed back to New York. As I mentioned, I experienced severe pain and pressure in the head while at our stop in Harrisburg, and I thought I was going to die on the spot. My wife took charge of driving us back home to upstate New York. Hard panic attacks began and I did not know what to do. From my cell phone I called our doctor's office to see if I could stop by and get some medication. I guess I knew deep down that the doctor had to see me before he would prescribe medication. Yup! That was the message that the nurse relayed to me. I went into more panic attacks, knowing that I could not get something right away. Boy, was it hard to swallow and to keep myself composed and in control!

On another occasion my wife had planned, several months before any of this happened, to go to a ladies conference. I was trying to be brave as I told her to go, but as she drove out the driveway, severe panic attacks hit me like a ton of bricks. I ran out of the house in desperation and flagged her down. A person's helpmate, family and friends are hemmed in because of another's condition and circumstances. Needless to say, my wife turned around, came back and was with me all the time. There are several ways to have a loss, but a loss causes grieving, disappointment, bitterness and anger. Some of this is hard to explain and accept as it happens. I experienced these things and I really didn't understand why.

We owned a twenty-four foot pontoon boat and I would cover it up for the winter. It was spring and I wanted to uncover it and get it ready to put into the water. It took all of my energy to go outside and do that, trying to avoid as much stress and panic as possible. Even to this day, ten years later, there are times it is somewhat hard to get out of bed and get going. Back then it seemed that everything I wanted to do was difficult and I was fearful to take a step forward. I believe it was because I did not know what was coming next, what the day would be like.

In May each year our town would have a paddle fest. This is where they displayed and sold canoes and kayaks. Every year our church parking lot would get jam-packed with people and vehicles. Since we lived on the property, the only place I could retreat to was our large back porch which overlooked the waterway. Our two-story house stood between me and the business of the parking lot. As I stood on the back porch, my panic attacks increased as the vehicles and people invaded the parking lot, which I considered my space. I felt trapped and isolated with really no way out. As I heard more and more of the crunching of the tires on the stony driveway and the many voices of people, the intensity of my panic increased. As in most cases I describe here in this chapter, it was so hard to swallow.

One mile from our house was a grocery store where we had shopped dozens of times. It seemed everywhere I would go, because of the panic attacks, it became a new adventure for me. My wife and I went into the store and it was totally different for me. The panic and stress would immediately kick in. It seemed like I was being hemmed in and things were caving in on me. I followed beside and behind my wife just a little. I felt insecure and afraid of what might happen. I held her arm and did not let go. I felt like a child holding onto his mother. I know it sounds weird, but that is truly what happened. Meeting people that I knew felt as if I were meeting them for the first time, it was hard and awkward. As we neared the cash register, there were people ahead, behind and to the side of me. I felt trapped and with nowhere to go. When I left the building and got outside, I felt better. It still affects me the same at times now, depending on the day.

It was very hard entering the church building where I pastored as well as any other church building. The crowds would send me into panic and stress attacks and I would have to leave. To this day I can only stay in church for one service, then I have to leave.

Another time I developed a severe panic attack was in a construction zone in our town. We had two vehicles, a car and a pickup truck. We had to take the car to the mechanic's for repairs. My wife was ahead of me with the car and she made it through the construction zone. They stopped me to wait for oncoming traffic. Oh boy! did the panic attacks come full throttle, the peddle to the metal. I felt trapped, I couldn't swallow and I felt like getting out and running, to where I don't know. I had to do everything in my power to stay calm and collected.

Once we entered a Home Depot store and, as big as it was, I felt like the tall storage shelves were going to come crashing down on me at any moment. I stepped outside and, like other times, felt some relief.

Three years prior to my severe panic attacks, I could not force myself into an elevator. I always took the stairs and used the excuse that I needed the exercise as my motive. I did need the exercise, but that was not my motive. Back in the 1970s I was in a large elevator in a hospital with a doctor and some employees. The elevator got stuck between two floors and my panic attacks started. Fortunate for me, the doctor in the elevator began ripping at the doors to pull them apart and my attention was drawn away from me and toward him. After 2001, I was on the road to my recovery. I stepped into an elevator, rode to the third floor, got out and realized I didn't have any panic attacks. I do not recall if I asked the Lord to take them away, but I'm so thankful that He did. He is an awesome God and I have learned to praise Him in the good times as well as the bad.

In the Fall of 2001, I received a phone call from my daughter at 2:00 a.m. She said her husband wasn't doing well. He was contemplating suicide as a result of his father passing away the previous October. He just could not handle the fact that his father was gone. They were very close and did a lot of work together. This was going to be my first night out by myself since my sleep deprivation. My wife could not go because we had two foster boys she needed to be there for. As I traveled the eleven miles to their house, I was praying and pleading with the Lord to open my son-in-law's heart to receive Christ as his Savior. When I arrived, he was on the phone with his mother in Florida. When he got off the phone, he dashed through the kitchen and living room, hugging me and saying, "help me, help me!" My first thought was to get him some counseling but as we walked to the sofa and sat down I said to him, "Would you like to receive Jesus as your Savior just like your father did?" My son-in-law said "yes" and right then he received Jesus into his life. When people don't respond to God in the good times, He sometimes sends trials our way so that we will come to Him. The next evening we met and he said as a result of Jesus coming into his life, a huge burden was lifted from his shoulders. That weight was his sin. Burdens are truly lifted at Calvary.

As I drove home that night I was rejoicing and singing in my pickup about my son-in-law's salvation. As I got excited, my panic attacks came back and I couldn't swallow. I had to stop singing and calm myself down. To this day when I'm around several people at a time I get mild panic attacks and clumsiness accompanies it. I find times, whether in the house, automobile or wherever, when I will yawn, it's not because I'm tired, but I'm having a small panic attack. Most of the time, I can't tell you why, it's just an automatic thought that comes into my mind. I chew gum, stop what I'm doing, go for a drive, redirect my thoughts, or go off to be by myself to help relieve the panic.

Shortly after my son-in-law's salvation, he showed me two verses from the Bible. *"You have tested my heart; you have visited me in the __night__; You have tried me and have found nothing; I have purposed that my mouth shall not transgress... I have __called__ upon You. For You will hear me, O God; Incline Your ear to me, And hear my speech"* (Psalm 17:3,6)

The following is a note that my son-in-law sent to me a couple of months after his salvation:

Dear Bob,
Just wanted to drop you a line to let you know that I am very thankful for helping me in my time of need.

For that I will always be grateful. I also wanted to let you know that I enjoy coming to your church and learning the Lord's word. I'm learning a lot, but I have a lot to go. I read every night and enjoy it tremendously. If you ever need someone to talk to, do not hesitate to call me. You have done that for me, the least I could do is return the favor. I know there are times that you would probably like to walk away from the ministry, but you're very good at what you do. I'm glad that I have you for a father-in-law.

Lord bless you,

SBG

CHAPTER 4

SLEEP DEPRIVATION

In the early stages of my depression, sleep departed from me. I could only manage two to three hours of sleep during a twenty-four hour period. There were several nights I had to sleep outside. It was April in upstate New York. At that time of year, the temperatures still get down to freezing. What sleep I could get was on a glider swing on our back porch. I would put on warm clothes, a hooded sweatshirt, joggers and blankets. Both in my bedroom and on the back porch, I would string up Christmas lights to give the area a calm, soothing atmosphere. Just writing about this, ten years later, brings back a lot of uneasy feelings. I would like to pause here and say that during those years of heavy depression, I would try different things, like the lights, medicines, or avoiding stressful situations to find relief. Sometimes it worked and other times it had no effect. A person needs to experiment to see what works for them.

As a result of my sleeplessness I would walk the church parking lot all hours of the night. I would put on my joggers, a hooded sweatshirt and a robe which I called my Joseph robe because it had many colors. The church building and parsonage were nestled in a wooded area, outside the reach of the street light and it was pitch black. As I walked facing the church building, I looked at the stained glass windows which engulfed the front of the church building. In one of the stained glass windows was a cross, as well as a cross on the steeple. The cross reminded me of Jesus who died for me and God's great love in sending Him. As I looked at the cross I would think, "Lord, will I ever make it through this awful season of depression?" I purposed in my mind and came to a conclusion that I would. My God is in control of everything and every minute of my life. As time passed, I would look at those crosses and pray, "Lord, if You want me to be here, I will and if You don't, I will move on as you direct." I did stay for three more years.

I left the church in good standing. I then accepted another pastorate forty miles away and I remained there for six more years before retiring. I purposed to get better and I did. I eventually came out of the most critical time of my depression. My encouragement to you is that you can as well. I feel that I will always face, to some degree, stress and depression. It's a matter of control and avoiding the circumstances that cause it that will keep me from deep depression.

Because of my constant walking, inability to eat right and sleep deprivation, I lost fifty pounds in a very short period of time. I was told this was dangerous to my health. Because of this trauma to my head and body, my vision became a little blurred. If you would take a pair of weak bifocals and look at the leaves of a tree, that was how my vision was. I tried to keep busy by fixing my own meals and while in the kitchen and dining room, my vision was blurry.

There was a reason why the Lord put me through this trial. One reason was that I would always have a clear, clean mind and conscience before God and man. Finally, ten years later, I have reached that goal. Slow learner, I guess. This comes through confessing our sins. I John 1:9 says, *"If we confess our sins, He is faithful and just to forgive us of our sins and to cleanse us from all unrighteousness."* And John 15:3 says, *"Now you are clean through the Word which I have spoken to you." (KJV)*

My wife and I, upon the recommendation of our spiritual counselor, I took a trip to Ohio to resolve some issues I had with my father. Any time I traveled very far from home and stayed overnight, it was difficult. It was like going into new territory and, with the lack of sleep, it was unknown and scary as what might happen.

I had a full-fledged woodworking shop. I spent a lot of time there, especially at night during my absence of sleep. It was very hard working in the shop after my recovery. I used it as a source of relief from my stress and depression, but I found I could not work in the shop. Once we moved I had it set up and well organized in my new garage, but I could not work there. Once what was a pleasure to me, was now stressful and overwhelming. Once what I always wanted now became a burden. I eventually made the decision to sell the tools and I have not regretted it.

The same is true with the new home we had. It was my dream home come true but the upkeep was too much for me. Our move to Florida, going to the ocean, enjoying the warm sunny days and writing replaced what I gave up.

Not many of the material things mean much to me anymore. I have a greater concern for that which is spiritual, witnessing to the lost and encouraging the saints to live for the

Lord. Individuals who are going through this life are dealing with stress, depression and a host of other ailments, but there is also a spiritual warfare constantly going on. Satan is trying to keep the unsaved from knowing Christ and he wants to keep the saved from living a victorious life for Jesus.

I love writing my experience in the tribulations that I went through in the hope that it might be a help to someone else. Ten years ago, God laid the title of this book on my mind. I talked about writing this book for the past ten years, as several people encouraged me to do so. Now in the spring of 2011 I am finally writing. I don't know how or in whose hands this will fall, but if one person is helped, to God be the glory.

CHAPTER 5

FALLEN SOLDIER

May God bless the U.S.A. and the men and women who serve in its military. Hundreds come home from the military with Post Traumatic Stress Disorder (PTSD). Sad to say, there are hundreds of soldiers who commit suicide. The key to initiating help is realizing that the person is suffering and he/she needs help. Just because he needs help, though, doesn't mean he has to seek psychiatric care or medication. He may just need patience. He may need a friend to listen to him. He may need time to adjust to civilian life. He may need a job to take his mind off of things. Try talking to him. If he communicates his fears, great. You are better off than most. But many who suffer from PTSD don't want to talk about it, think about it, address it. Don't force him. Be patient. A USA Marine named Ryan says, *"Courage is the*

ability to face adversity, even if it's within yourself" (from How to Help an Iraq Veteran With Depression).

J. R. Martinez, who just won the most recent "Dancing with the Stars" competition, was invited to the Pentagon for a meeting. A Pentagon spokesman called J.R. and told him that he demonstrated the strength and resilience of a wounded veteran. The 28-year-old J. R. was severely burned over more than 40 percent of his body when the Humvee he was driving for the U.S. Army struck a land mine in 2003 (Yahoo News, Nov. 25, 2011). Just like J. R. and hundreds of other military personnel have successfully overcome, so can you. If you don't know Jesus as your Savior, I invite you to trust Him today (See. Chapter 13). As Christians, we are in the Lord's army and we are on the winning side.

In II Timothy 2:3,4, the Bible says *"You therefore must endure hardship as a good soldier of Jesus Christ. No one engaged in warfare entangles himself with the affairs of this life, that he may please Him who enlisted him as a soldier."*

During the summer of 2001, I had to take a four and a half month sabbatical because of my depression. The stress and strain of the pastorate was too much for me. I had to have time to recover. Before I go any further, I want you as my readers to know that the church continued to pay my salary and support us with their prayers and compassion. The church and friends shared their concerns through verbal communications, letters, cards and phone calls. I know the people did not have a full understanding of what was happening. Nor did I. However, they stuck with me offering their faith, mercy and compassion. My wife and I thank the church from the depths of our being for their love and generosity. One of the largest healing factors is to know people care.

During that summer I did a lot of walking while listening to soft music on my CD player. One evening as I was walking, I was headed downtown, dressed in warm clothes, listening to my music. On the corner of Main Street and our street was a business. As I walked by on the other side of the street, the owner from his front porch called me over to chat with me. I've known him and his family for about eight years. We talked for about five minutes and then I was on my way. The next day about noon, a knock came to my door. It was the gentleman with whom I'd had a brief conversation the evening before. I was on our back porch swinging on the swing. My wife invited him to come and visit with me there. He sat with me and began to share what was on his mind and the reason for his visit. As we talked, he shared with me that he could not sleep the previous night thinking about my condition. He informed me that by looking in my eyes, he saw my traumatized condition, stating that I looked like one of the soldiers who returned home from the Vietnam War in a depressed state.

On the church property there were three buildings: the church building, the parsonage and a ministry house called the cottage house. This house was and is still today being used for pastors, missionaries and other folks in Christian ministries as a getaway for rest and vacation. A pastor and his wife, who we knew prior to their staying there, came out to meet us when we returned home from town. We chatted for a few minutes, then went on our way. When the pastor and his wife went into their house, she shared with him that they needed to have us over for a visit. Soon we went to their house and she shared with me that she could tell I was in deep depression just by looking into my eyes. She had gone through a major depression several years earlier. We talked for a long time and it was comforting to know that someone else had gone through the same thing and made it through. On a few occasions, we visited in their home for a getaway and rest. We talked again about our experiences with depression and my wife and her husband learned new things about how severe the stress and depression were. I hope this book of my dealing with depression will be of help to the person who is or will be going through depression.

I met another gentleman in our town park as I was walking and we walked together for a distance. He pointed out to me that I was like the point of an arrow, taking the full brunt of the tragedies that took place in our community by all the counseling I had done. I thought to myself that I was like a cowboy at war with the Indians being struck with an arrow, wounded and yet surviving.

I had returned to the pulpit in September of 2001. It was good to preach again and I felt clean and free in my delivery. My wife said that I had more boldness in my preaching. My praise, honor and glory go to Jesus, my Savior and God. I love Him with all my life. Just a few days after getting back into the pulpit, the 9/11 terrorist attacks took place in our country. This was a little setback because of the mass number of deaths that took place. Also, I had thoughts of disbelief and anger for what happened. How could this happen in America? One year later, I was asked by a neighboring town to have a part in the firemens annual convention. This was the one-year anniversary of the 9/11 attacks. This was a memorial service for the families and victims of those attacks. They asked me to speak as a clergyman in the community. People in our town and the neighboring towns knew that I had been wounded and laid aside for a period of time. About three hundred people were at the memorial service. During the ceremony, a photographer was taking pictures of the day's events. I noticed that as I was speaking he knelt down and took a picture in an upward direction. When our local weekly paper was published, it had a picture of my Bible in the forefront, and me speaking. I believe, to the community, the picture was used by God to say the minister and the Word of God is back! To my God belongs glory and great praise for wonderful things He does. The man has recovered from his medical condition.

To be truthful, it was hard coming back and at times it still is. That day after speaking, my wife drove us out of town to rest from the day. It took me eight hours to prepare that 15 minute message, with one of our foster boys giving me flack before we left for the service, constantly being around people and then the delivery of the message left me with a lot of head strain and panic. Ten years later I still have some difficult moments with some panic and head strain. It's not always easy, but the trials down here cannot be compared to the future glory we will experience in Heaven. In Romans

8:18, the Bible says, *"For I consider that the sufferings of this present time are not worthy to be compared with the glory which shall be revealed in us."*

The next thing I want to mention is the thing that hurt me the most. I came to the realization that I could not continue pastoring while in my present condition. I shared with the folks that I needed time to rest and heal from my present clinical and physical condition and depression. One Sunday morning it was made known that I had something to say. I walked alone to the front of the church and announced to the people that I had to take off some time. Later that morning, a godly man in the church said to me that he felt that one or more of the deacons should have walked with me. It's the worst feeling in the world, feeling alone in a crowd. Now I know to a small degree what Jesus and His servant Paul experienced. I also felt rejected, deserted and helpless. When I arrived at the back of the auditorium, I said something to my friend who was also a deacon and although now I don't remember what it was, I do remember that he physically turned his back on me. At that point he took power and control of leadership. It was like a knife piercing my heart. From then on, the deacons, except for one, turned against me instead of being a help to me. The one deacon who stayed true is still a deacon today and a very close and respected friend. He is an excellent teacher, preacher and godly man. If a friend does not understand what another person is going through, if he is a true friend he still does not turn against him.

I remember one Wednesday evening during our Bible study and prayer time, when the time came to divide up into groups for prayer, I noticed the head deacon pointing in a secret way motioning the other deacons to meet downstairs. At that point I felt something might be up. As time passed, I went over to the church office just to make my presence known, to see how things were going. To my surprise and hurt, the deacons handed me a rough draft of a paper outlining the qualifications for a pastor. Talk about being rejected, wounded, knocked down and left for dead, figuratively speaking! How that arrow of pain pierced my heart.

They also gave some opinions what should be expected of a pastor's wife. My wife and I both had so many mixed feelings. Instead of feeling safe and protected, we felt rejection, bitterness, anger and continued depression. As we discussed issues relative to this matter with our counselor, describing the various situations, the more we could see control issues surfacing. Periodically my wife and I would meet with the deacons to see how things were going and to give a report on my progress.

If I had to do it over again, I would not have met with the deacons. It was a wrong decision. As we met and various things were discussed, my anger would get out of control. I should have waited until I felt a little better. Even one of the folks in our church suggested I should have found a place to go for a few weeks. Looking back on it now, I believe I would have healed much faster. Later I did meet with each deacon individually to ask forgiveness and see how we could move forward. I took counseling from a few pastor friends of mine on whether I should resign or stay. They all said I should stay and get things resolved and I did.

When some of our people found out about my treatment by the deacons, they were really upset. We had several prayer warriors in our church and they prayed that the Lord would bring us back to unity again. I knew that because of their prayers everything worked out and I was able to pull through. Three years later, God, in His timing, called me to another church. Thank you, Lord, for great deliverance.

Soon after I got back into the pulpit, we had a business meeting. Two deacons came to that meeting with an agenda. I don't know what it was, but one deacon deserted the other.

Later we had a deacons meeting and gave each deacon a turn at voicing his opinion and concerns. The one deacon who stayed for the business meeting, shared with us in the deacons meeting that he thought I should resign but if I did not he would serve under my leadership. To my knowledge we arc friends today and I have much respect for him.

Believer, we are in a fierce battle with Satan and his demons. Do not retreat but move forward, defeating the foe in Jesus' name. The Apostle Paul describes this spiritual warfare in Ephesians 6:10-17 when he admonishes believers to be strong in the Lord and the powei of Ilis might and to put on the whole armor of God in order to withstand the wiles of the devil. We need to be girded with truth, wearing the breastplate of righteousness, walking in the peace of God, carrying the shield of faith and wearing the helmet of salvation. Most importantly, we need to be praying always in the Spirit. If you are a Christian, you are engaged in a spiritual battle of universal proportions. Your soul is in conflict against the forces of evil, so fight the good fight. As frightening as the power of darkness may appear, you serve the God of light, and the victory is His!

Words of Encouragement from the Bible, God's Word

Believer, no matter what befalls you, listen to what the Apostle Paul said in Philippians 3:12-14: *"Not that I have attained, or am already perfected, but **I press on**, that I may lay hold of that which Christ Jesus has also laid holed of me. Brethren, I do not count myself to have apprehended; **forgetting** those things which are behind, and **reaching forward** to those things which are ahead, **I press** toward the goal for the prize of the upward call of God in Christ Jesus."*

CHAPTER 6

EMOTIONAL TRAUMA

L isten to her scream. My sister, on occasion, would experience a nightmare. She would stand up in her bedroom and scream during the night. It was an ear-piercing scream, a horrible noise. I do not think it bothered her, for she was asleep. For the rest of the household, it was a traumatic experience. I don't know about the rest of the family, but for me it was hard to get back to sleep. During my time of depression I faced several emotional traumas.

The <u>first</u> emotional trauma was Anger. I cannot tell you why I had anger but I can tell you I did experience it. You have heard the phrase that goes something like this: "That person sure has a short fuse." I displayed, several times, a short fuse during my first year of depression. One Wednesday evening prior to our Bible study and prayer, a few of us were talking about taking a nap during the daytime. Someone was kidding and said something like this: "You don't need to take a nap." As soon as they said this, I immediately got angry, stomped out of the church building, slamming the door. Anybody who knows me knows I like to have fun. Normally I would have joined in on the fun.

Remember, this was during the darkest time of my depression. I had sleep deprivation and it really affected my whole being. I believe this person was kidding, but back then it was hard for me to discern what was serious and what was fun. No matter how hard I tried, it was very difficult not to get angry.

On another occasion we were headed for my counseling session, ninety miles away. Part of the trip meant getting on a four-lane highway. Up to this point, my wife had been doing all the driving. The reason: I couldn't stand the pressure of being behind the wheel of a vehicle. I felt a lot better at this point in time and I decided to drive. I did fine until a car came up close to me at a faster rate of speed than I was going. They pulled out quickly and went around me. Suddenly I found myself in a panic mode and just like throwing a switch, I was filled with anger. I wasn't ready to drive in traffic. Today I have no trouble at all driving in traffic.

It seems the ones I lashed out at were family members. My wife and family have endured a lot and I praise the Lord they still love me. In the last few years there were times I would get angry because I let myself get too tired. I have to say to myself, "Robert, back off, be silent for now." At times I got grouchy, mean, snapped at people and, on a few occasions, went into a full-fledged rage. This usually happened to family members, the ones who love you the most. I really have that anger under control now. I'm being honest and open with you, no sugar coating.

The <u>second</u> emotional trauma was Crying. I am a very emotional person to begin with and if something touches my heart, tears flow. If I'm at a parade and I see the American flag, hear the band playing the national anthem and I hear the noise of emergency vehicles, I cannot carry on a conversation. I'm so choked up with emotions I cannot speak.

The first few weeks around our place, you could see me crying often. Emotions inside me swelled up to the point I could not control the crying. In the counselor's office, there would be times I would break down and cry. Just like with anger, I could not understand why I cried but I did. It was a great relief once I did cry.

Our health center was right next to the church. The last couple of years of pastoring was getting to me. The stress of leadership was getting harder. Every time I went to the church to do administration and study, the back of my head would be in pain. It got so bad that at times I would call the health center and the doctor would take me right in. The doctor was a Christian and she would encourage me in the faith, not before releasing my emotions through crying. I praise the Lord for this doctor's encouragement.

For folks who have depression, getting out, is very hard. I preferred going to a secluded place so as to not face the trauma of getting out and being busy. My wife and I thought it would be good to go and visit my son and his family. The trip took us about two hours. I had a good day. It was getting late in the afternoon and we decided it was time to return home. Before we left, my son and his family said they would like to take us out to supper. He took the lead and we followed. As we went to the restaurant, they saw a garage sale. My son pulled over to the side of the road and suddenly I went into panic mode. With my stress and panic attacks, when someone did something unexpected I would go into panic mode. By the time I'd pulled up behind his vehicle, I was sobbing. No matter how hard I tried, I couldn't stop. It was so traumatic and embarrassing for me. Instead of going to dinner, we left for home. This was such a rough time but my God is so good. He is in control and knows exactly what is going on. Thank you, Father, for bringing me back to health.

The third emotion was Fear. I read that someone took the time to search in the Bible for how many times the words "fear not" and similar expressions appear. Not surprisingly, but just like our God, the number is 365, one for each day of the year! Even if this is not totally accurate, it is definitely close.

I had a fear of taking pills, no matter the size and any new prescription. Previous to this I had no problem taking medications. I was afraid to get up in the morning. Again I cannot tell you why but I was. I was afraid to move without having my Bible reading and prayer time in the morning. No matter where I was, I had to spend that time with the Lord. I was afraid to go someplace new. It was very, very difficult. I had what I will call mixed fear. At times I was afraid of dying and there were times I was not. After I got back into the pulpit, I felt very bold, confident and my assurance was firm. I now believe I was under spiritual attack with the attempt to cripple me in my walk with the Lord. When

I woke up during the night I would be afraid I could not go back to sleep. I was afraid to travel for fear of the unknown. Prior to my trip to the valley of depression, these fears did not exist.

The <u>fourth</u> emotion was Sadness. Everyone gets sad sometimes – a brief blue mood, disappointments, grieving after losing a loved one, etc. When sadness is exhibited for some time, it probably means one is depressed. The depression is not just a case of the blues. It is a serious medical illness often caused by an imbalance of chemicals in the brain.

CHAPTER 7

EXCRUCIATING STRESS

The siren at the fire house is blaring. The flashing lights from the fire trucks illuminate the night sky as they move to the location of the fire. Upon arrival, the firemen feel the intense heat from the flames. As the water is applied to the building, the fire is soon extinguished. There is damage to the house structure but it is spared.

In April of 2001, because of the stress in my life, my arms were burning. I would wake up at night and my arms and shoulders were burning so badly that the only thing missing was the flames. This continued for several nights. The days I walked to the church across from the parking lot, my body would burn with stress. People or no people in the building, the burning was present. I tried to attend as many services as possible during my sabbatical time in 2001. I stayed as long as I could but many times I had to leave because of the intense burning.

My daughter lives some seventy miles from us. One Sunday I attempted to attend their services. As I entered the foyer and then the auditorium, the stress and panic attacks hit me. My daughter came out to be with me and soon we went to her house. To feel better I remained outside. When I would be alone, the stress was less.

This excruciating stress happened to me over and over again. I spoke to my counselor about attending a week-long Bible conference. He said it would be fine but to only stay as long as I could bear it and then leave and return home. I had a drive within me that I was going to get through this stress and depression, not letting it conquer me. The conference had three to four Bible studies per day. The auditorium would have 300-400 people in attendance. As soon as I would enter the building, my whole body would begin to burn with stress plus I would have small panic attacks. I sat in the back of the auditorium for the Bible study. After one and a half hours I would go back to my room and take some medicine for my stress. I would sleep most of the afternoon. I could only attend one service per day. When we would go to the dining room for our meal, the stress and panic attacks would begin again. I stayed the whole week of the conference. At my next appointment with my counselor, he was really pleased that I was able to stay there the whole week.

There are days that I still feel some stress in my head, shoulders and elbows. I believe everyone has some degree of stress and the key in living with it is control. I control my stress by removing myself from whatever is causing it. For the next nine years of pastoring I suffered from this time of major stress. Now, a year since my retirement, most of that stress is gone. When I do feel it coming on, I change what I'm doing, get outside, go someplace if I have to and take medicine to relieve it, remove myself from what causes the stress. God is so good. He brought me through the fire. Praise His holy name!

Here are the lyrics to the song "The Refiner's Fire", words and music by Jon Mohr and Randell Dennis, which are a powerful reflection of what I experienced during this time:

There burns a fire with sacred heat, while hot with holy flame, and all who dare pass through its blaze will not emerge the same. Some as bronze, and some as silver, some as gold, then some with great skill all hammered by their sufferings on the anvil of His will. Their learning to trust His touch to crave the fire's embrace, for though my past with sin was etched, His mercies did erase. Each time His purging cleanses deeper, I'm not sure that I'll survive, yet in growing weaker keeps my hungry soul alive.

Chorus: the refiner's fire has now become my sole desire. Purged and purified, that the Lord be glorified. He is consuming my soul, refining me, making me whole. No matter what I may lose, I choose the refiner's fire.

Following are some things that helped me with my stress. The <u>first</u> is that when I felt overwhelmed by stressful situations, I would spend time listening to soft music: classical music, or music from nature, for example, the ocean sounds, thunderstorms and rain, the sounds of running water and the loon. The music had a positive effect on my brain and body.

<u>Second</u>, when I felt overwhelmed, I would talk to my best friend on this earth, my wife. There were dear friends of ours who attended our church in the summer time. A member of the family was suffering from stress and depression. We would periodically call one another to see how we were doing. That connection was a tremendous help in my healing. Find a true friend who will accept you as you are.

They will listen to you even though they do not understand. *"A friend loves at all times..."* (Proverbs 17:17). *"A man who has friends must himself be friendly, But there is a friend who sticks closer than a brother"* (Proverbs 18:24).

Find someone who is a true friend and who will listen. I had a close friend halfway across the country. He had bouts with stress and depression like I did. Again, it would be encouraging to share with one another, but I tried not to contact friends too much. I knew that I had to stand on my own to grow stronger. In the beginning of my depression, I thought the doctors could do all the work for me to get through this awful time. I found out soon that it is my battle and I must go through it to come out the other side refined and purified.

The third technique I used was, when I felt overwhelmed and I was not able to talk to someone, I would talk out loud to myself. I would ask myself why I was stressed and depressed. At times when I walked, I lifted my hands toward Heaven and I talked out loud to my Heavenly Father. I did not worry what people thought, even though from appearance they might have thought I was crazy.

We, as mankind, tend to judge according to the outward appearance rather than knowing the facts. In searching for a king over Israel, Samuel the prophet thought that a certain son of Jesse, David's father, would be king. *"But the LORD said to Samuel, Do not look at his appearance or at his physical stature, because I have refused him. For the LORD does not see as man sees; for man looks at the outward appearance, but the LORD looks at the heart"* (I Samuel 16:7)

Most of the time I walked in the country. Not many people would see me raising my hand or talking to the Lord with outstretched hands. But if I was in fellowship with my Heavenly Father I was oblivious to my surroundings. I cared what my Heavenly Father thought and what He was doing in my life.

The <u>fourth</u> thing that helped was an article I read in "Healthline: Connect to Better Health" magazine from October 1, 2011 which says that eating the right foods can reduce stress. "Stress levels and a proper diet are closely related. Unfortunately, it's when we have the most work to do that we forget to eat well and, instead, resort to using sugary, fatty snack foods as a pick-me-up. Try to avoid the vending machines and plan ahead. Fruits and vegetables are always good, as is fish with high levels of Omega-3 fatty acids, which have been shown to reduce the symptoms of stress. A tuna sandwich really is a brain food." (www.

healthline.com/health-slideshow/10-ways-to-relieve-stress/ eat-right)

Number <u>five</u> is that through counseling I learned that when I have stress, I need to practice slowing down my breathing. I would go off by myself, usually in the backyard on a sunny day in a chair and just relax. I would close my eyes, breathe deeply in and out and just relax. This practice really did help. Another thing I do, no matter where I am, I will place my hand over my eyes and just relax.

The <u>sixth</u> is that when I feel overwhelmed, I try to laugh. I love to have fun and one of the best stress releases is laughter. I'm told that laughter decreases our stress levels. It tricks our nervous system into making us happy. Psalm 126:2a says, *"Then our mouth was filled with laughter and our tongue with singing, ..."* And Proverbs 17:22 says that *"a merry heart does good, like medicine, But a broken spirit dries the bones"*.

The <u>seventh</u> thing I would do when I felt overwhelmed was to meditate. I did not meditate on nothing, I meditated on the Bible, God's Word. I mentioned in a previous chapter that I would memorize portions of the Bible to keep my mind sane. The Bible, God's Word, is both comforting and healing. *"Blessed is the man who walks not in the counsel of the ungodly, Nor stands in the path of sinners, Nor sits in the seat of the scornful; But his delight [joy] is in the law of the Lord, And in His law [the Bible, God's Word] he meditates day and night"* (Psalm 1:1,2). The next verse says that the person who meditates on God's Word will prosper.

The eighth thing I would do when I felt overwhelmed with stress is to change the activity I was engaged in at the time. I would stop what I was doing for a few minutes, or go out for a drive, talk to people, take a hot shower or go for a short walk. Even to this day I have times where it is hard to get out of bed. Sometimes I think this happens because I do not want to face the day with its stressful situations. I have to tell myself to get up, get dressed, get breakfast, get out of the house, get going. I try to get my mind focused on others and not on myself.

My number nine activity when I feel overwhelmed and stressed is to get proper rest. I need between 8 and 10 hours of sleep a night. When I had sleep deprivation in 2001, I found it caused a lot of problems and stress. This vicious cycle of no sleep caused my brain and body to get out of whack and it only got worse with time. I believe I was in danger of losing my life from sleep deprivation. I needed help and that's when I went to my doctor. He prescribed medication to help me sleep. Before I retired from the pastorate, because of the stress of the position, I needed 10 to 12 hours of sleep plus a nap in the afternoon. Presently I sleep about eight hours and I generally do not take a nap in the afternoon. I try to work through the day which makes me tired plus take a small dose of medicine that keeps me asleep. I manage my time so I can get my proper rest.

And finally, the number <u>ten</u> thing I do when I feel overwhelmed and stressed is to try to learn how I can deal with it. Stress is an unavoidable part of life. Too much stress can cause potentially serious physical and mental health problems. How well I know. I have a built-in indicator. Just above my left elbow I will experience burning when I am under too much stress.

Encouragement from the Bible, God's Word

"Hear my cry, O God; attend to my prayer. From the end of the earth, I will cry to You, when my heart is overwhelmed, lead me to the rock that is higher than I." (Psalm 61:1,2)

"I cried out to God with my voice—to God with my voice; And He gave ear to me. In the day of my trouble [affliction] I sought the Lord; my hand was stretched out in the night without ceasing; My soul refused to be comforted. I remem-

bered God, and was troubled; I complained, and my spirit was overwhelmed. Selah." (Psalm 77:1-3)

"I will love You, O LORD, my strength. The LORD is my rock and my fortress and my deliverer, My God, my strength [lit. my rock], in whom I will trust; My shield and the horn [strength] of my salvation, my stronghold." (Psalm 17:1,2)

CHAPTER 8

LONG, LONESOME VALLEY

I told myself to take a hike and that's what I did. At the time I took that hike in the Adirondack Mountains, a microburst had gone through leaving a forest full of downed trees. I was halfway through my walk when I slipped, spraining my ankle. It was a long, lonesome journey back to my vehicle. I thought I would never get back.

In my state of depression, it seemed that I would never get back to my health again. I would walk and walk and walk several times a day. I just could not be around people and confusion. It would cause stress and deepen the depression. On my walks I carried and played a CD player. I would take extra CDs and batteries. I played soft, relaxing music which comforted me. At times the batteries went dead and for some reason that put me into a panic mode. At this point of my depression, these things were necessary, not optional. During the spring and summer months of 2001, I lost fifty pounds and my eating was erratic. As I walked in town, people would walk or drive by me, honking their horns, smiling and waving. From the outward appearance, people thought I looked fine, but inside I was hurting and very lonesome. This is why living with depression is so exasperating.

In the cool of the springtime I wore warm clothes and a hooded sweatshirt. Next to the church was a park. I would walk in the park a lot. One day as I was walking I found a golf ball at the end of the ball field. As I walked I found more golf balls. All around the park was woods. I would go beyond the tree line and guess what I found—more golf balls. I did this for several days in a row and I would find at least one golf ball. I found about fifty golf balls in all. I was a little confused as to how they got there because the golf course was a little more than a mile away. To my knowledge, I do not know of anyone who can hit a golf ball a mile. My conclusion is that God placed them there somehow to keep my mind occupied.

The journey of depression is long and lonesome, but I pushed on and I pushed on hard with the attitude that I was going to triumph. In the good times and the bad times, God is always with us. God says, *"...I will never leave you nor forsake you"* (Hebrews 13:5b). As I walked the sidewalks and country roads I would memorize Bible verses. This would refresh my mind and I was renewed spiritually. Over the course of the summer I learned over two hundred Bible verses. I would get so restless and unsettled in my mind, whether at home or visiting my family, that I had to go for a walk to find relief.

This is what would make me so lonely as I walked through this depression. To this day I still need alone time, but nothing like I needed at the beginning of my depression. I know and serve the living God and as I walked the sidewalks or the country roads I would do so with hands lifted, praying to my Heavenly Father and asking for deliverance from my affliction. Today I do not have to plead with God like I did then, because He has delivered me. I spend quiet time every day thanking my Heavenly Father for His goodness to me.

During this season we had a foster child and were required to attend a meeting. The meeting was being held about ninety miles away. As we sat in the crowded dining room I was getting stressed and having panic attacks. I eventually had to go outside and walk with my music playing to calm down. Oh how lonesome the valley!

My purpose in recording my own accounts of depression is to give insight to those who are experiencing depression themselves as well as to their caregiver(s). As a result of going through depression myself, I can understand what one goes through. I felt so alone when I walked the church parking lot all night long. I felt so alone when we had family reunions, because of not being able to spend quality time with family and friends.

Several times during the very hard time of my depression I would enter the church building, lay prostrate on the platform, crying out to God for help and deliverance. God, in His time, delivered me from my long, lonesome journey. Today as I write, I am down by the riverside at a picnic table. Ten years ago I would sit at the same picnic table pleading to God for deliverance. God is in control, I give Him the glory for all things and I trusted Him for what He was doing in my life at that time.

One more thing I would like to share with you in my lonesome valley experience – As I was walking, big dark gray cold clouds filled the sky. As I walked I was quoting a verse from the Bible which says, *"Draw near to God and He will draw near to you"* (James 4:8). As I quoted that verse I looked up at the clouds and there was an image of a person in a white garment. I do not believe anyone else could see what was visible to me, but it was a mental picture in my mind. It was a confirmation of the Bible verse I had been quoting.

There were times I prayed to God my Father to have an angel appear to me to comfort me and let me know that God was present. No angel appeared but I just knew in my heart, as said in God's Word (the Bible), that God and His angels were present. If you do not know Jesus as your Savior, maybe He is allowing affliction in your life so that you might come to know Him in a personal way, as your Savior. If you do know Jesus and you are going through affliction, it is a good indication that God is working in your life.

I'd like to quote an article from the *National Liberty Journal* called "Helping the Hurting" by Dr. Edward Hindson, Assistant to the Chancellor of Liberty University, dated June 8, 2002. Although it is lengthy, I believe you will find Dr. Hindson's words very helpful.

Everybody has problems. We can't get very far on
the road of life without encountering them. Sooner

or later we all face challenges and difficulties which push us to the limits of our ability to cope.

The message of the Bible is one of help for the hurting. In its pages are the greatest resources in all the world. These timeless truths have stood the test of endurance generation after generation. Instead of new theories and experimental "solutions," the Bible offers solid advice based upon the inspired truths of the Word of God. These truths tell us that God alone can and will help us deal with our problems.

The Bible reminds us that God is greater than our problems. Since He rules the universe, He can overrule every circumstance of life for our own good. Romans 8:28 reminds us, "We know that in all things God works for the good of those who love him, who have been called according to his purpose."

The very fact that you are going through a difficult time may be the greatest indication that God is at work in your life. Rarely do we learn the deep lessons of life when everything is going well.

The real learning comes when everything goes wrong. That's when God usually gets our attention. When the bottom falls out of our lives and there is nowhere else to turn, we will find ourselves instinctively calling on God for help. There is something basic to human nature that drives us to God when we come to the end of ourselves. Even unbelievers will cry, "God help me!" when faced with a crisis.

While we experience the blessings of God in our daily lives, life is not without its difficulties, challenges, and struggles. The Bible reminds us that God comforts us in our troubles, not necessarily from our troubles (II Corinthians 1:4). In fact, suffering and trouble are His methods of shaping our lives and our character. In some cases, God may use the worst of circumstances to accomplish the best of results for our own good.

CHAPTER 9

ASCENT TO VICTORY

Hope came on August 5, 2010 for thirty-three Chilean miners trapped one-half mile underground. Through modern technology, a twenty-six inch shaft was drilled down to the miners and they ascended to the surface in a narrow, twenty-one inch wide capsule. The most vulnerable men were taken up first. They had grown weak and sickly in the brutal underground conditions of 90-degree heat and 90 percent humidity. They had survived their worst nightmare (ABC News 11/30/11). Just like these men were delivered from a horrible pit, you too can be delivered from the dark pit of depression.

David, who penned most of the Psalms, reveals to us from his own experience what it is to go through stressful and depressing times. I found so much comfort in reading the Psalms. I recommend that anyone in depression read the book of Psalms. David, in recording his own life, opens up his heart to us and was very open to what he was going through. David's faith in the Lord during times of affliction, trials and depression is what took him from the valley of depression to the mountain of victory. My Lord did the same for me and I am certain He can do the same for you as well. *"I waited patiently for the LORD; And He inclined to me, and heard my cry. He also brought me up out of a horrible pit, out of the miry clay, And set my feet upon a rock, and established my steps. He has put a new song in my mouth [praise to our God); many will see it and fear, and will trust in the LORD. Blessed is that man that makes the LORD his trust"* (Psalm 40:1-4).

Following is a list of things that brought me from the valley to the mountaintop. It is my prayer that these will help you.

The <u>first</u> thing I did was to have a mindset that I was going to get better. I said *I will triumph*. Positive thinking lifted me up and gave me hope. Negative thinking pulled me down and gave me a sense of hopelessness. My positive thinking focused on the Lord and others. My negative thinking focused on me.

I remember looking out of our big picture window that faced the church. With everything that was going on in my life and in the church, I felt overwhelmed. In my mind I pictured a very high wall between the church and our house. I pictured the wall so high there was nothing I could do to get over it. It was then I said, "I will triumph," "I will overcome," "I will have victory in my life." "The Lord will be my strength and deliverer," and He was.

When I returned to the pulpit in September 2001, I felt clean, free, strong, bold and triumphant. The mind is a very powerful thing. *"For as he [man] thinks in his heart [mind], so is he..."* (Proverbs 23:7).

I will use a personal illustration to show you what the mind can do. Between my junior and senior years of high school, I met my wife-to-be. During my senior year she had a couple of opportunities to visit me in Ohio. Instead of staying home from school the day she was arriving from New York state, I would keep saying in my mind that I have a headache. As time went by my headache came and grew worse. I went to the nurse's office and told the nurse I had a headache. She told me that I looked a little pale and that I should go home. Once back at home I reversed the process and eventually I had no headache.

Our minds are very powerful. I learned from counseling that if I would find a quiet place, relax my mind and think on something pleasant, things would feel better. Usually I would sit in the sun, close my eyes and think on one thing. I usually thought on the sounds of an ocean or the running waters of a river. Also I would close my eyes and quote Scripture in my mind. *"Rest in the LORD and wait patiently for Him"* (Psalm 37:7). *"Now thanks be to God who gives us [me] victory through our Lord Jesus Christ"* (I Corinthians 15:57). *"Now thanks be to God who always leads us in triumph in Christ, and through us diffuses the fragrance of His knowledge in every place"* (II Corinthians 2:14).

The second thing I did to get better was to take my medication. We live in a great age of advances in the medical world. I do not like taking medications but there are times doing so is necessary for recovery. To date I have been able to lessen the dosage and am not taking as much as I was in the beginning of my stress and depression. I would like to get off the rest of my medicine some day. In the future I hope I can, but if not, I need to accept the fact that I might have to be on some for the rest of my life. If it makes me lead a better life, I will not be afraid to do so.

The <u>third</u> thing I did to get better was to make necessary changes in my life. My wife and I ministered in churches for forty-two years. Our ministry was going into churches with very low attendance and building them up to where they could financially support a pastor. With that said, I had to work outside the church to support my family. On July 25, 2010 I retired from the church as pastor. I had run out of energy. This change in my life was hard. I left the pastorate and the people I loved. Financially it was a strain. After forty-two years of doing the same thing, I felt at a loss.

I am now retired from pastoring, but not from ministry. New doors of opportunity have opened. Presently I have the opportunity to write this book. My prayer is that this book will minister to many thousands of people. My God is so good. *"Show me your ways O LORD, lead me in truth, teach me, for you are the God of my salvation, on you I wait all the day"* (Psalm 25:4,5).

The <u>fourth</u> thing that I did to help me get better was for me to read and memorize the living Word of God. In the beginning of my depression I could not read or listen to the Word of God as it was being taught, but I could memorize Bible verses. When we read the Bible, it is God speaking to us; when we pray, we are speaking to God. Our God is living and so is His Word. *"For the Word of God is living and powerful, and sharper than any two-edged sword, piercing even to the division of soul and spirit and of joints and marrow, and is a discerner of the thoughts and intents of the heart"* (Hebrews 4:12).

I do not know how people make it through life without knowing God in a personal way and His precious Word. I clung to Him and the Bible. I was encouraged by several individuals who personally visited me and shared their experiences with depression and how they survived. I realized I was not alone in this battle with depression. Just as I was encouraged by others, I too want my ascent to victory to be a help for those going through this difficult season. Folks would talk with me on the phone and give me positive feedback that I was going to make it through this deep valley of depression and I did! Praise the Lord!

People would send me cards and letters expressing what God was doing in my life. The reason for storms and trials in our life is to make us stronger. God is like the potter, molding and shaping us to do His will. Today, I feel like the vine that was pruned by the vinedresser, removing excess "stuff" from my life so that I might be more available to serve Him.

I received the following letter from a pastor friend of mine who was a guest speaker a couple of Sundays in my absence from the pulpit in 2001. "Thank you for the privilege of filling your pulpit while you were away. My wife and I had a wonderful time getting to know your people and renewing some old acquaintances. Your people are responsive to the gospel and speak highly of you and your ministry. There is no doubt in my mind whatsoever that your people love you and are fully behind you in their prayers for you and your wife at this time in your life. We know the Lord's hand is on you and your ministry" – R.A.P.

The next is a letter that was sent to me by an individual who was facing the same difficulties at the same time I was. I quote this letter in part and what it said I humbly accept and give Jesus my Savior all the glory. "Dear Pastor Stoudt: I have wanted to write to you to express just a bit of my thanks to you for all you have done for a long time. I finally have a minute to collect my thoughts. I sometimes wonder if the Lord has taken you through this trial just so that I could look at a great man of God [in His, i.e. God's, strength of course] and be encouraged. Your consistent seeking after the Lord is so precious to my husband and I to behold. Whom have I in Heaven but thee [Jesus]. We both know that we have no place to go but to God." – P.B.S.

I was so uplifted by visits, phone calls and letters from friends who are my brothers and sisters in the Lord. God so many times ministers to us through people so we can say, *"God is our refuge and strength, a very present help in trouble"* (Psalm 46:1).

The words of a poem by Annie Johnson Flint echo my sentiments too:

He's helping me now this moment,

Though I may not see it or hear

Perhaps by a <u>friend</u> far distant,

Perhaps by a <u>stranger</u> near,

Perhaps by a spoken message,

Perhaps by the printed word;

In ways that I know and know not

I have the help of the Lord.

The <u>fifth</u> thing that helped me to ascend to victory was learning to laugh again. Laughter is good for anyone. I always have loved to laugh. I like to make other people laugh even if it is at my own expense. Going through the deep valley of depression I lost my laughter, but now it is back again and how I praise the Lord for it. I'd like to share a lengthy quote from Help-Guide.Org, a trusted non-profit resource: "Laughter is the best medicine. Humor is infectious. The sound of roaring laughter is far more contagious than any cold, sniffle, or sneeze. When laughter is shared, it binds people together and increases happiness and intimacy. In addition to the domino effect of joy and amusement, laughter also triggers changes in the body. Humor and laughter strengthen the immune system, boost one's energy, diminish pain, relax muscles, and protect us from the damaging effects of stress. Best of all, this priceless medicine is fun, free, and easy to use. Laughter is a powerful antidote to stress, pain, and conflict. Nothing works faster or more dependably to bring one's mind and body back into balance than a good laugh. Humor lightens one's burdens, inspires hopes, connects us to others, and keeps us grounded, focused, and alert. There are definite mental health benefits of laughter. It adds joy and zest to life, eases anxiety and fear, relieves stress, improves mood, and enhances resilience. The social benefits from laughter include strengthening relationships, attracting others to us, enhancing teamwork, helping defuse conflict, and promoting group bonding." The Bible says, *"A merry [includes laughter] heart does good..."* (Proverbs 17:22). Coming to the close of 2011, I am finding myself doing things I thought I would never do again. The journey has been long but Jesus has been with me every step of the way.

Encouragement from the Bible, God's Word

"I can do all things through Christ who strengthens me." (Philippians 1:13)

"Wait on the LORD; Be of good courage and He shall strengthen your heart; Wait, I say, on the Lord." (Psalm 27:17)

"But those who wait on the LORD shall renew their strength; They shall mount up with wings like eagles, they shall run and not be weary, They shall walk and not faint." (Isaiah 40:31)

CHAPTER 10

WHY AM I GOING THROUGH THIS AFFLICTION?

The first thing we will do is define the word 'affliction'. Affliction is a state of distress, a circumstance that is hard to bear; physical, spiritual or both. Synonyms for the word affliction are: trouble, trials, tribulation, pain and suffering. Surprisingly to many people, sometimes a person goes through affliction because they are living correctly. Another reason for affliction may be because of one's disobedience to the Lord. Going through affliction is a plan of God to humble us so that we can continue to be used of Him, avoiding pride. When God allows us to experience affliction, suffering and pain, He is preparing us so that we can comfort and connect with another person going through the deep, dark valley of depression. Finally, perhaps God is revealing to a person their need to be saved.

At some point, I believe, all of us will eventually experience affliction, to one degree or another. Hopefully, we will look at the above-mentioned reasons for affliction on an individual basis from a biblical perspective. When we are afflicted there is One who knows our exact pain and suffering and that is God. There are times that other people know, perhaps not fully.

My valley of the deep, dark depression brought me just short of death and going home to be with the Lord. My affliction happened because I overextended myself in ministering to people who had lost their loved ones and friends through death. I was told later that I and the church should have called for outside help to counsel these individuals. I also learned other things that helped me in my walk with the Lord. It is a lot easier talking about it than going through the depression. Since I did go through the deep, dark valley of depression, I can understand what others are going through.

One thing I know is that God is in control of my life and that He was and is always with me. Hebrews 13:5b says, *"...I will never leave you nor forsake you."* I have purposed to be steadfast no matter how hard the affliction. *"Therefore, my beloved brethren, be steadfast, immovable, always abounding in the work of the Lord, knowing that your labor is not in vain in the Lord"* (I Corinthians 15:58).

Friend, if you are going through some affliction, I want to encourage you to push forward. I know this may be hard for you to do, but you *can* overcome. God tested me to see if I would stay true to Him and I have. *"Create in me a clean heart, O God, and renew a steadfast spirit within me"* (Psalm 51:10). God still has a plan for me upon this earth and I wait upon Him to lead me. For the moment He wants me to write this book. This book is a testimony of how I went down to the deep valley of depression, stayed on the bottom for some time and then ascended to the mountain of victory.

This month, November 2011, I can say that I am just about all the way back. To do so I had to press forward and get my mind busy and occupied with other things and God has blessed wonderfully. He can bless you the same way. Praise the Lord!

On Thanksgiving morning of 2001, at 5:00 a.m., at my sister's house, God gave me the title for this book – "My Valley of Depression, Mountain of Victory." For ten years I have shared with family, friends and counselors my desire to write this book and they shared with me that it is a book which needs to be written. Now is the time and I believe it is from the Lord. My desire is that God would use it to encourage others to become victorious in their life.

If you are not a born again believer, I want you to know that God may be using your affliction to bring you to Himself. Read Chapter 13 of this book to know how you can be saved. I mentioned at the beginning of this chapter some reasons why a person might go through affliction. I will illustrate this from the Bible. Remember, the people I cite lived the present and had no idea what the outcome would be. We have the advantage of looking back at these people as we read their accounts in the Bible and we see the beginning to the end. The same way is true with us; when we go through affliction, we do not know what the outcome will be, but God does and He will see us through.

First, a person may go through affliction for doing good. I am going to use an Old Testament character by the name of Job. Please read chapters one and two of this book of the Bible. Job was a man who *"...was blameless and upright, and one who feared God and shunned evil"* (Job 1:1b). There was a day when Satan came into the presence of God with the other angels. The Lord said to Satan, *"From where do you come?"* (Job 1:7a). So Satan answered the Lord and said, *"From going to and fro on the earth, and from walking back and forth on it"* (Job 1:7b). Then the Lord said, *"Have you considered My servant Job, that there is none like him on the earth, a blameless and upright man, one who fears God and shuns evil"* (Job 1:8). Job was a godly man and he was doing everything right. The Lord has recorded for us twice the godly character of Job. Job was a very special man, one whom the Lord could trust to pass the test that He allowed Satan to put Job through. Satan told the Lord that He had put a hedge of protection around Job and he knew that he could not touch Job without God's permission. Satan attacked Job's character by saying to God, *"...stretch out your hand and touch all that he has and he will surely curse you to your face"* (Job 1:11). Satan attacked Job's family, killing all his children and their families. What a painful, painful loss. Satan attacked the wealth of Job. In those days wealth was measured by how many animals and servants one had. All the servants died except the one who returned to let Job know what had happened. Family, servants and animals dead. Job's response was, *"Naked I came from my mother's womb, And naked shall I return there. The LORD gave, and the LORD has taken away; Blessed be the name of the LORD"* (Job 1:21). Scripture records that *"In all this Job did not sin nor charge God with wrong"* (Job 1:22).

Satan was not finished afflicting Job. However, The Lord again commented to Satan about Job's character. Job had lost everything he had but the Lord says to Satan, *"... he still holds fast to his integrity, although you incited Me against him, to destroy him without cause"* (Job 2:3b). Three other things happened to Job. Satan was allowed to touch his body and Job was struck with painful boils. Then Job's wife said to him, *"Do you still hold fast to your integrity? Curse God and die."* (Job 2:9). Imagine! I would like to think that as godly as Job was, his wife and children were also as godly, but his wife's comment does make me wonder. Nonetheless, it was very painful, I'm sure, for Job's wife to see her husband in this extreme affliction, pain and suffering. Going through affliction is extremely hard on the one going through it, but it is very hard on that person's family and friends as well. Then Job said to his wife, *"You speak as one of the foolish women speaks. Shall we indeed accept good from God, and shall we not accept adversity?"* (Job 2:10). In all this, Job did not sin with his lips.

The last thing we see is Job's friends turning on him. The great majority of the book of Job is a back-and-forth conversation between Job and his three friends Oh, how lonely and secluded Job must have felt, but he stayed true to his God. What is your affliction? I know it is very, very hard but God knows what He is doing. Like Job, trust Him and remain true and faithful to Him no matter what. I know He can bring you through this painful affliction.

Second, a person may go through affliction because of disobedience. My illustration for this is the Old Testament prophet Jonah. The Lord tells Jonah to go to Nineveh *"...and cry out against it; for their wickedness has come up before Me"* (Jonah 1:2). Jonah refused and his actions demonstrated that as he fled from the Lord's presence in a ship going to Tarshish, in the exact opposite direction he was directed by God to go. Therefore, the Lord brought a great tempest upon the sea. The sailors said, *"Come, let us cast lots, that we may know for whose cause this trouble [affliction] has come upon us"* (Jonah 1:7). Then Jonah admitted that it was because he had fled from the Lord. They asked him what they should do and he said, *"Pick me up and throw me into the sea and the sea will become calm for you. For I know this great tempest is because of me"* (Jonah 1:12). The sea became calm after the sailors did as Jonah said, they threw him overboard.

God had prepared a great fish and Jonah was swallowed and he was in its belly three days and three nights. *"Then Jonah prayed to the LORD his God from the fish's belly. And he said, I cried out to the LORD because of my affliction and He answered me"* (Jonah 2:1,2). Not only was this person afflicted because of his disobedience, but others (the sailors on board the ship to Tarshish) were affected as well.

The path of affliction can be very lonely. Both Job and Jonah faced loneliness, one for doing good and being godly and the other for being disobedient.

Third, God may allow a person to go through affliction to keep them humble, so that pride does not enter in. In the New Testament, the Apostle Paul represents an example of this. Paul said, *"and lest I should be exalted above measure by the abundance of the revelations, a thorn in the flesh was given me, a messenger of Satan to buffet [beat] me"* (II Corinthians 12:7). Paul's "thorn in the flesh" is not identified with certainty. It is greatly understood to have been a physical problem. Whatever it was, it was both painful and humiliating. Paul continued, *"concerning this thing [affliction], I pleaded with the Lord three times that it might depart from me. And He said to me, 'my grace is sufficient for you, for my strength is made perfect in weakness.' Therefore I take pleasure in infirmities [affliction], in reproaches, in needs, in persuasion, in distress, for Christ's sake. For when I am weak then I am strong"* (II Corinthians 12:8-10).

Beware of doing things in your own strength, for it can lead to self-reliance. Glory in your weaknesses (affliction) for this can lead to humility and dependence upon God. He can show Himself strong through your weaknesses (affliction) and demonstrate to the world what He can do through a willing servant. God gives strength and weaknesses (affliction); let Him work through both.

Once I returned to the pulpit after four and a half months away, folks said there was more power and boldness in my preaching. Oh how I praise my Savior and Lord Jesus Christ. It is very, very difficult going through affliction but I can assure you from my personal experience that Jesus will see you through. *"But thanks be to God who gives us the victory through our Lord Jesus Christ"* (I Corinthians 15:57). I try to use the Bible as much as possible because God speaks and strengthens us through His Word. King David wrote most of the Psalms and they show the struggles he had and his dependence on the Lord. May we be willing to do the same.

Fourth, a person may go through affliction to become a comfort to others. *"Blessed be the God and Father of our Lord Jesus Christ, the Father of mercies and God of all comfort, who comforts us in all our tribulations [afflictions] with the comfort which we ourselves are comforted by God. For as the suffering of Christ abounds in us, so our consolation [comfort] also abounds through Christ. Now if we are afflicted, it is for your consolation [comfort] and salvation [deliverance]..."* (II Corinthians 1:3-6a). After my experience of deep depression, I was approached by a gentleman who shared with me the affliction he was going through. I said to him, I understand exactly what you are going through. He gave me a questionable look, so I shared with him my journey through affliction. He acknowledged that I was really able to understand his situation. Yes, I've been there, done that. The nine more years I was a pastor following 2001, I was able to use my experience to help others deal with their affliction. I was not afraid to be transparent and open about my depression. So many people were helped by it.

The fifth reason a person may go through affliction is for salvation. When a person is down at the bottom of affliction, there is no place to look, but up. They look to God for help and deliverance. Turn to Chapter 13 and learn how you can have hope, eternal hope. Jesus wants you to live with Him forever, in Heaven, a place of blissfulness. He wants to be your Savior.

Perhaps you're familiar with the poem "Footprints" by Carolyn Joyce Carty. I've included it here because it speaks to the way in which God so gently deals with us and helps us through our affliction.

Footprints

One night a man had a dream.
He was walking along the beach with the Lord.
Across the sky flashed scenes from his life.
For each scene he noticed two sets of footprints
in the sand: one belonged to him,
and the other to the Lord.

When the last scene of his life flashed before him,
he looked back at the footprints in the sand.
He noticed that many times along the path of his life
there was only one set of footprints.
He also noticed that it happened at the very
lowest and saddest times in his life.

"Lord, you said that once I decided to follow you,
you'd walk with me all the way.
But I have noticed that during the most troublesome
times in my life there is only one set of footprints.
I don't understand why when
I needed you most you would leave me."

The Lord replied, "My precious, precious child,
I love you, and I would never leave you
during your times of trial and suffering.
When you see only one set of footprints,
it was then that I carried you."

A Mountain to Climb

The mountain stands before me,
I must face it every day.
But I'll not turn around
And I'll not run away.
Though painful it may be,
I know it's truly for my best,
And as I climb, through wearily,

I know I'll pass this test.

For God is with me every step

And sends His grace abundantly,

And I am certain in my heart

It's God's will meant for me.

Though filled with pain and sorrow,

I will face the climb each day,

And Know my God is with me

And He will show the way.

Whatever mountain you may face,

Take heed to these words true,

And know if God is there for me,

He's there and loves you, too.

Gina Laurin

CHAPTER 11

THINGS THAT HELPED ME

The following are things that helped me in dealing with my depression. I had to experiment to find out what worked and what did not work for me. Everyone is different and we all need to find out what works for ourselves. I say this graciously and kindly, but I did not let others dictate to me what worked or did not work. I learned to say No. I tried to be aware of what bothered me and I would remove myself from that stress.

Climate Change:

When the weather changed from a nice sunny day to a rainy day, my head would pain. Before I went through my depression, I would get headaches when the barometric pressure changed. In the years following my depression,

I have had to learn the difference between barometric and depression headaches. Living in upstate New York, the seasons were very distinct and drastic in their change. When a cold front would come through, my head would hurt for two weeks, then clear up. There was a woman in our church who would call me on occasion and say, "PB [Pastor Bob], do you have a headache today?" When I said yes, she would be relieved.

Change in Elevation:

The forty-mile trip from the mountains to my daughter's place was a distinct change in elevation. Going through the deep time of my depression, my wife had to drive because the slightest change in elevation would give me head trauma. Going those forty miles was torture. Today, the elevation change does not bother me. On occasion I still have pain in the back of my head and when I discontinue what I'm doing, then it clears up.

Confusion:

I define confusion as a *disorganized* noise. Confusion still bothers me today. It may be a group of people all talking at the same time. I'm at the park today sitting at a picnic table. There are several different noises I'm hearing all at the same time. They are loud traffic noise, people talking about different subjects and children playing and screaming. Exit stage right. I leave. Once, in front of our house, three motorcycles were in an accident. It was unexpected, with people screaming, hurting and traffic stopped. I could not deal with it. I have learned to avoid confusion as much as possible.

Commotion:

I define commotion as *organized* noise. At my last pastorate, we would have game night every so often. We played a game called bonco. There were four tables with four people at each table. There was a lot of talking but everyone was talking about some area of the game. This I refer to as *organized* noise or commotion. No matter how hard I tried, as time passed I needed to remove myself from the noise. A lot of my quiet time comes when I take a drive by myself. I can only stay a short time at family gatherings. Fortunately, my wife and children understand. Now that I have recovered from panic attacks, I like being left alone. The quiet time is very healing for me.

Crowds:

Indoors or out, when I get in crowds I get very jittery and antsy. I feel like I'm walking on my tiptoes and I tend to get clumsy. When people are around me at the counter of a fast food restaurant I get very awkward. When I count money with people around, I become 'all thumbs'. Many times my wife goes to the restaurant counter to pay for the food while I find a seat. To overcome this problem, I remove myself from crowds as much as possible. Solitude is a good solution for me, but I'm careful not to become too isolated. Daily, to one degree or another, I have to motivate myself to go where people are. I will probably have this the rest of my life and that's okay. I will adapt.

Conflict:

Conflict is not always avoidable, but I try to avoid it as much as possible. As pastor there were times, both with individuals and groups, I would face conflict, differences that we had. I believe it bothers anyone to a certain extent, but one with stress and depression is bothered to a much greater degree. Being a leader of the church, there was no avoiding disagreements. I was worn out to the point where I could not handle any part of the pastorate, hence retirement.

Crying:

In the midst of my stress and depression, I would cry a lot. As the expression goes, I would cry at the drop of a hat. Crying gave me release and I would feel better afterwards. I did a lot of crying at home, in the doctor's office and during my visits to my counselors. Even today there are times I feel so overwhelmed I could cry and sometimes I do. In another chapter of this book I mention some of my experiences with crying. My advice is not to worry what people say or think; cry, it gives release.

Chewing Gum:

When I am under stress I tend to clench my teeth and jaw. Most of the time I do not recognize that I'm even doing that and then I end up with a headache and head pain. It took me a long time to figure it out. Once I figured it out, I tried various things to see what would relieve the stress in my head. Finally, I figured out that chewing gum would keep my jaws moving and my teeth from clenching, thus relief. At first I thought it was the depression. Today I carry gum with me, lots of gum. Driving was one of the big culprits. After a short time of driving I would become aware I had a headache, from not chewing gum.

Cloudy Days:

Many places in America have cloudy days a large portion of the year. The part of the country we lived in had cloudy days, day after day, week after week. The people who had lived in this area all their lives had trouble with depression during the winter months. Florida is called the Sunshine State. We have had the opportunity to move to Florida. It is the best move I've ever made. The sun shines most of the time and the heat is soothing and healing to me. There are times when I feel depressed and I go out and sit directly in the sunshine for about twenty minutes. The heat feels so good and it relieves my stress and depression.

Criticism:

No matter what you do in life, there is always someone who feels called to be a critic. Criticism can be very stressful, upsetting and destructive. I try to take what good I can from the critics and then forget the rest. In the past I had a tendency to let critics control me, but now I do not let those people influence me the wrong way. I will graciously back away and avoid that person.

Counseling:

Counseling is good. I had two counselors and they both were born again believers. One dealt with the clinical, the other with the spiritual. It is important to have the right counselor. I was taught how to control my anxiety, stress and depression. I was not ashamed at all to go to my counselors. I would go up to the window of the counselor's office, check in and receive my yellow slip for when I went into the counselor. I was not embarrassed or ashamed. Absolutely not. All I wanted was to get better. Through counseling, medication and determination I have ascended from the dark valley of depression to the mountaintop. My prayer is that you will, as well.

Concentrate:

Concentrate on others and not on yourself. When I dwelt on what I was going through, it made me feel worse. When I would reflect on others, it made me feel better. Get the outward look, not the inward.

I learned what helped me and I set as my goal to implement them. On the other hand, I try to avoid those things that hinder me. Since this is a chapter entitled "Things That Helped Me," I want to share some Scriptures about help.

Encouragement from the Bible, God's Word

"Behold, God is my helper; The LORD is with those who uphold my life." (Psalm 54:4)

"O God, do not be far from me; O my God, make haste to help me." (Psalm 71:12)

"Unless the LORD had been my help, my soul would soon have settled in silence." (Psalm 94:17)

"...the LORD is my helper; I will not fear what man can do to me." (Hebrews 13:6)

Dear friend, God *will* help you. I hope you receive encouragement from the following poem.

I refuse to be discouraged,

To be sad, or to cry;

I refuse to be downhearted, and here's the reason why:

I have a God who's mighty, Who's sovereign and
supreme;

I have a God who loves me, and by grace I'm on His
team.

He is all-wise and powerful, Jesus is His name;

Though everything is changeable, My God remains the
same.

My God knows all that's happening; Beginning to the
end;

His presence is my comfort; He is my dearest Friend.

When sickness comes to weaken me,

To bring my head down low,

I call upon my mighty God; Into His arms I go.

When circumstances threaten to rob me of my peace;

He draws me close unto His breast, Where all my striv-
ings cease.

When my heart melts within me, and weakness takes
control;
He gathers me into His arms, He soothes my heart and
soul.
The great "I AM" is with me. My life is in His hand.
The "Son of the Lord" is my hope. It's in His strength I
stand.
I refuse to be defeated. My eyes are on my God;
He has promised to be with me, As through this life I
trod.
I'm looking past all my circumstances, To Heaven's
throne above;
My prayers have reached the heart of God, I'm resting
in His love.
I give God thanks in everything. My eyes are on His
face;
The battle's His, the victory mine; He'll help me win
the race.
I can do all things through Christ who strengthens
me!!!!

— by Lita Kurtzer

CHAPTER 12

EXCERPTS FROM
MY JOURNAL

There was a man and his name was Nebuchadnezzar, and he was King of Babylon. He made a golden image which was nine feet wide and ninety feet high. He caused the people to fall down and worship it. King Nebuchadnezzar *"...was walking about the royal palace and he said, 'Is not this great Babylon, that I have built for a royal dwelling by my mighty power and for the honor of my majesty?' While the word was still in the King's mouth, a voice fell from heaven: 'King Nebuchadnezzar, to you it is spoken: the kingdom has departed from you! And they shall drive you from men, and your dwelling shall be with the beasts of the field. They shall make you eat grass like oxen; and seven times [seven years] shall pass over you, until you know that*

the Most High rules in the kingdom of men, and gives it to whomever He chooses. That very hour the word was fulfilled [Daniel's interpretation of the King's dream] concerning Nebuchadnezzar; he was driven from men and ate grass like oxen; his body was wet with the dew of heaven till his hair had grown like eagles' feathers and his nails like birds' claws. And at the end of the time I, Nebuchadnezzar, lifted my eyes to heaven, and my understanding returned to me; and I blessed the Most High [God] and praised and honored Him who lives forever." (Daniel 4:29-34) *"At the same time my reason returned to me, and for the glory of my kingdom, my honor and splendor returned to me. My counselors and nobles resorted to me. Now I, Nebuchadnezzar, praise and extol and honor the King of heaven, all whose works are truth, and His ways justice. And those who walk in pride He [God] is able to put down."* (Daniel 4:36, 37)

God put Nebuchadnezzar through affliction so that he would know there is only one God. That God is in control of everything and there is none greater than He. The King was humbled from his pride. There were times I felt like Nebuchadnezzar, being put out to pasture so He could do a work in my life. His understanding and reason departed, and when he had learned his lesson, his understanding returned.

Today you might be going through affliction because God wants to reveal Jesus to you, the one who is the Savior. As a Christian, God wants to prune you, take things out of your life that keep you from serving Him. God will show you what He is doing if you just let Him. I know I have more compassion and understanding for those who are going through depression as a result of my experiences. My trust in the Lord has grown deeper. People mean more to me than material things. I am freer to serve Him. Look for what He is revealing and teaching you. God loves you and so do I. Just like Nebuchadnezzar made it through and was restored in understanding, reason and position, you too can make it through. I know you can..

I am going to break this chapter from my journal excerpts into two sections. The first covers the time that I was out of the pulpit for four and a half months in 2001. The second section deals with the years following my return to the pulpit (2001-Present 2011). As I read through my journal, I see things clearer now than when they happened.. I leaned on the Lord a lot, especially in the beginning of my journey downward. I went over a lot of Scripture and spent much time in prayer. My days were not the same. Some days I felt good. Other days were just a struggle to get through. When

I talk about good days, it does not mean I was well, but that the stress, depression and panic attacks were at a lower level. Each day was a struggle, some were just harder than others. Sleep was hard to come by. I pastored for nine more years after 2001. That held me back from getting better sooner, but God was so good to me.

This **first section** of Excerpts from my journal explains the beginning time period of my problems that led to my pulpit absence for several months in 2001.

April 25, 2001

I had a huge panic attack. One of the men in the church had to come and stay with me for about three hours. I did get a good night's sleep, it took a while getting to sleep, but I did sleep.

April 26, 2001

Nice sunny days. I had a good rest the latter half of the night. Each night I go over God's Word memorizing scripture. God is answering my prayers. Thank you, Lord. Today I did a lot of work. This afternoon I had panic attacks and a hard time all evening. I felt closed in. I hope I get a good night's sleep. I did not get to sleep until 3:00 a.m. with the aid of medicine.

April 27, 2001

I slept until 9:30 a.m. Again I went over some scripture. Today I go to see my counselor. We left home at 11:00 a.m., returned home at 7:00 p.m. Through counseling I learned how to control panic attacks. Doing it is another thing, it's not easy. I did have a good evening. I did some work in my workshop.

April 28, 2001

I had an excellent night. Once in the early morning I felt the stress coming on and I was able to control it. While in my workshop, I felt sick to my stomach. The rest of the day I felt bad and I cried a lot. As evening came, I got so much worse.

May 4, 2001

I had a very good night's sleep. Yesterday and today is beautiful. Warm sunny days help me a lot. I took sleep medicine last night to get a good night's sleep. Sleep is so vital to my healing process. I was good until about 2:00 p.m. My daughter and her children came over. They are very, very good kids, but at once I felt some panic; it lasted until later in the evening. When I have changes in my daily routine, it causes stress and panic. *[Note: As I'm writing this book today, November 1, 2011, I have some pain in the back of my head. This is the result of going back ten years and rehashing things that happened to me then.]*

May 14, 2001

I had a good night's sleep with the aid of some sleeping medicine. My daughter and her children were here today. Then we went to our other daughter's place in the evening for supper. I had a hard time. I still need my wife with me.

May 18, 2001

I had a good night's sleep. We left at 8:00 a.m. for a counseling session with my spiritual counselor. It takes two hours to get there. My wife and I had a very good meeting with the counselor. I had a few panic attacks, but I'm okay. My wife and I are alone tonight. We plan to get a good night's sleep. My blood pressure has been good. I did get a good night's sleep.

May 30, 2001

I went to my counselor. I had a very good visit.

June 4, 2001

I had a fairly good night's rest. Late morning and afternoon I worked, but I felt out of it. I was so bad I thought I was going to go crazy. My wife called the doctor and he gave me some medicine to relax me. I had a very restful evening. *[Note: This is the time period where I had severe sleep deprivation and I didn't know if I was going to live or die.]*

June 12, 2001

Good night's sleep. Took a two-hour trip to see my spiritual counselor, good session. I took a nap. I feel good when I lie down. I woke up with a headache, back of the head pain and stress in my arms.

June 18, 2001

We are at our daughter's place. I had a very good night's sleep. I took no sleep medicine. I took a walk on a country road. I hauled some firewood in my pickup for my daughter. I went to town and did banking and I went into a few other stores. I felt a little uneasy in the evening.

July 17, 2001

I had a good night's sleep. I went to the doctor, he increased my depression medicine. I drove an hour to Home Depot and picked up a washing machine. I went back to our daughter's and from there went to the fair. It was stressful because I saw older folks with gray hair and it reminded me of death *[as you may recall, it was dealing with death that put me into my depression]*. My wife and I stayed overnight at our daughter's. We went home the next day.

July 23, 2001

My wife and I drove fifty miles to a beach on a large lake. We spent the day with our families. I had to do a lot of walking because of the stress and depression.

August 9, 2001

Today I had an appointment with my counselor. My wife and I visited a family from church. I did a lot of talking today. I had a hard time with stress, depression and assurance.

August 28, 2001

I had a good night's sleep. I had a very busy day. I woke up early and spent time in prayer. I studied in preparation for my message the upcoming Sunday, September 9, 2001. From April till now, I've spent every day dealing with some level of depression, panic attack and stress.

September 9, 2001

I had a good night's sleep. Today I preached for the first time in four and a half months. I believe it went okay. Thank you, Lord. I did some reading and then went out on the boat. I could only stay fifteen minutes in the evening service. One of our deacons was scheduled to speak. Today was a good day overall. Praise the Lord!

The following is found at the conclusion of the daily devotional by Radio Bible Class called *Our Daily Bread*, dated October 12, 2011. Dennis Fisher wrote that day's devotional and after he'd written that "Sometimes we find ourselves in what feels like a hopeless valley without the strength to go on," there's a short poem and a quote to ponder on:

When circumstances overwhelm
And seem too much to bear,
Depend upon the Lord for strength
And trust His tender care.

—Sper

"When we have nothing left but God,
we discover that God is enough."

Perhaps this poem says it best. It's from *"Streams in the Desert"* by L.B., August 9, 2001.

I have been through the valley of weeping,
the valley of sorrow and pain;
But the "God of all comfort" was with me,
At hand to uphold and sustain.
As the earth needs the clouds and sunshine,
Our soul needs both sorrow and joy;
So He [God] places us oft in the furnace,
the dross [impurities] from the gold to destroy.
When He leads through some valley of trouble,
His omnipotent [all powerful] hand we trace;
For the trials and sorrows He sends us,

Are part of His lesson in grace.

Oft we run from the purging and pruning,

Forgetting the gardener knows,

that the deeper the cutting and trimming,

The richer the cluster grows.

Well He knows that affliction is needed;

He has a wise purpose in view,

And in the dark valley He whispers,

"Soon you'll understand what I do."

As we travel through life's shadowed valley,

Fresh springs of His love ever rise;

And we learn that our sorrows and losses,

Are blessings just sent in disguise.

So we'll follow wherever he leads us,

Let the path be dreary or bright;

For we've proved that our God can give comfort;

Our God can give songs in the night.

This **second section** of Excerpts from my journal begins the years following 2001. I continued pastoring nine years subsequent to my 2001 depression. In those nine years I still had bad days but many were good as well. In 2009 and 2010 I was getting worse. My depression, panic attacks, and stress were recurring. The cause was being in leadership in the role of pastor and all its responsibilities. I soon had to resign as pastor. On July 25, 2010 I tendered my resignation, which read as follows:

July 12, 2010

Dear Church Family,

At the end of 2009 I approached the deacons and let them know they should begin looking for a new pastor. I would soon be retiring because of medical issues. At this time the pastor search committee was formed to begin looking for a new pastor.

Shortly after the pulpit committee was formed, I knew I could not fulfill all my responsibilities as pastor. I also shared with the pulpit committee and deacons that I would need help with some of the administrative responsibilities and jobs. It was agreed upon by all and I was relieved that I would have some help in these areas.

As time progressed the three deacons approached me and they shared with me their feelings that I needed a period of rest. They talked about a 3month sabbatical. I was so pleased that the deacons would consider this and present it to the church. It brought joyful tears to my eyes. One of the deacons said they would present it to the church at July's regular business meeting and that I would not need to be there. He said they would vote on it the following week.

Within the past month or so it has been increasingly difficult for me to be in the position of pastor. The deacons were concerned for me and we came to an understanding. I needed their wisdom to help see me through this decision. They have counseled me wisely.

I am formally resigning as of July 25, 2010. This will be my last Sunday preaching as your pastor. I think this is the wisest choice for me and you as my flock. I love you all so much! Thank you for taking care of me and loving me! I also want to thank you for considering to provide three months' severance pay. It would be greatly appreciated.

I want you to succeed and continue to grow. I pray daily about the new leader God has chosen for you.

With the love of our Savior,
Your pastor ... Robert Stoudt

Since my resignation as pastor on July 25, 2010, I have improved. I continued to improve after selling our house, moving to Florida and getting all the things done that go along with moving. We now live in a wonderful 55plus evangelical Christian community called Il Villaggio.

As I write this, in the fall of 2011, I feel really good. I am always going to be in recovery mode and I need to be aware of what I do. There are limitations. That's life. One of the things I need to do every day is to keep busy and keep my mind occupied. If I don't, I come under stress. Laying around thinking about things is not good. Get up, get out, get going, get busy – get, get, get. *"Blessed is the man whose strength is in You [God], Whose heart is set on a pilgrimage. As they pass through the valley of Baca [weeping], They make it a spring; the rain covers it with pools [blessings]."* (Psalm 84:5,6)

August 10, 2010

My wife and I went to the bank to fill out some paper-work. We picked up medicine from the pharmacy. I took someone to the Office of the Aging to a doctor's appointment forty miles away. From noon until I went to bed, I was having a very bad head day. I told my wife that I did not want to die but I did not want to live like this either. I broken down and cried. *[Note: after I slowed down and got my needed rest, I was okay.]*

November 12, 2010

My wife and I got up and did some errands. I packed some things for our move to Florida. We went to our daughter's for the day and I felt pretty good. It was a gorgeous day.

November 28, 2010

My wife and I attended the church from which I had resigned. A great message was delivered by the guest speaker. My wife and I spent the afternoon and evening together. I am beginning to feel much better. Thank you, Lord.

Fall of 2011

From the time of my resignation as pastor in July of 2010 until now, a year and a half later, I am feeling much better. Removing myself from stressful situations and my vocation as pastor, I am feeling much, much better. We all have some stress in our lives and as we learn to manage it we can live a better life. To God be the honor, glory and praise for what He has done in my life. I love Him so much and I want to be faithful to Him until I go to Heaven. He has certainly been faithful to me.

Elizabeth Kubler Ross says: " The most beautiful people we have known are those who have known defeat, known suffering, known loss, and have found their way out of the depths. These persons have an appreciation, a sensitivity, and an understanding of life that fills them with compassion, gentleness, and a deep loving concern. Beautiful people do not just happen."

Encouragement from the Bible, God's Word

"Through the LORD's mercies we are not consumed, Because His compassions fail not. They are new every morning; Great is your faithfulness." (Lamentations 3:22, 23)

"...Worthy is the Lamb [Jesus] who was slain to receive power and riches and wisdom, And strength and honor and glory and blessing." (Revelation 5:12)

"Great is the LORD, and greatly to be praised..." (Psalm 48:1a)

"He [God] gives power to the weak, And to those who have no might He increases strength." (Isaiah 40:29)

CHAPTER 13

ETERNAL HOPE

This book is about the personal trauma that I had with stress and depression. Many days I felt so helpless in my medical and clinical condition. There were days that I felt I had no hope of making it to the next day. So many in their depressed condition contemplate suicide for the purpose of ending the terrible experience they are going through. In one section of this book I shared that I told my wife, "I don't want to live like this," but I never once thought of ending my life. Instead, I knew there were medical, clinical and spiritual resources for me – and for you as well. Committing suicide not only hurts a multitude of people around you, but if one commits suicide without knowing Jesus Christ as personal Savior, suffering will continue for all eternity, never having an end to it. My hope is in Christ, I know Him as my personal Savior and when I die I will be in His presence in Heaven.

I never contemplated suicide for it would have dishonored my Savior Jesus Christ as well as hurt my family deeply. God's Word tells me that He will never give me any more than I can handle. *"No temptation [testing] has overtaken you except such as is common to man; but God is faithful, who will not allow you to be tempted [tested] beyond what you are able, but with the temptation [testing] will also make the way of escape, that you may be able to bear it"* (I Corinthians 10:13). God has a reason for allowing me to experience my depression and affliction. Although I may experience much pain and hurt in this life, the moment I die it will be all over and I will be in His presence free from all affliction.

As I begin this last chapter, entitled Eternal Hope, I pray that you will seriously consider what God says in His Word, the Bible, about salvation and living for God.

I would like to begin by asking three questions. First, would you like to go to Heaven when you die? Yes or No. Second, most people have their own idea of how to get to Heaven. What would you say: I would go to Heaven by good works, or being baptized, or by being a good Samaritan, or by joining a church, or by doing penance, or by being born again, or some other way? Third, do you believe the Bible is the Word of God? Yes or No.

In my 65 years of living upon this earth, I have never doubted the Bible. I had strong temptations to do so, but I did not yield to those temptations. Please read Psalm 119 and discover some precious truths about God's Word, the Bible.

Following, I'm going to share with you how to know Christ as your personal Savior and then how to grow in Christ once you are born again.

The Bible says, *"It is appointed unto men once to die..."* (Hebrews 9:27a). All mankind has one appointment that cannot be canceled, that is death. What does it mean to die? Man is made up of three parts: the body, soul and spirit. When we talk about death, it is when the soul and spirit depart from the physical, fleshly body. The body when dead decays and returns to dust. So, what happens to the soul and spirit when it departs from the body? They go to one of two places, one is called Heaven and the other is called Hell. Heaven and Hell are very real and literal places. One's eternal destination depends upon what one does with Jesus as one lives upon this earth. I want to share a few things with you about your eternal destination.

First, the Bible says **God loves you**. *"For God so loved the world [mankind] that he gave His only begotten Son that whoever believes in Him shall not perish but have everlasting life"* (John 3:16). God's love for you is unconditional no matter how good or bad you are. There are two destinations referred to in John 3:16. The first is evidenced by the statement that whoever believes in Him (Jesus) shall not perish. What does it mean to perish? The word means to destroy. It is the soul of man existing in eternal torment and separation from God forever with no chance of escape. *"So it was that the beggar died and was carried by the angels into Abraham's bosom [Heaven]. The rich man also died and was buried. And being in torments in Hell, he lifted up his eyes and saw Abraham afar off and Lazarus in his [Abraham's] bosom. Then he cried and said, Father Abraham, have mercy [compassion] on me and send Lazarus that he may dip the tip of his finger in the water to cool my tongue, For I am tormented in this flame"* (Luke 16:22-24).

Hell is real. Hell is a place of flame, torments, outer darkness and separation from God forever. *"The Lord is not slack concerning His promise, as some count slackness, but is longsuffering toward us, not willing that any should perish but that all should come to repentance"* (II Peter 3:9).

The next thing we read in John 3:16 is that whoever believes in Jesus will have everlasting life. Everlasting life is mankind existing in Heaven, a place where God and those who trusted His Son Jesus as Savior, will live forever. *"So it was when the beggar died and was carried by angels into Abraham's bosom [Heaven]"* (Luke 16:22a). Heaven is a place of blissfulness, a place where there is no separation from God. *"God Himself will be with them [believers] and be their God. And God will wipe away every tear from their eyes; there shall be no more death, nor sorrow, nor crying. There shall be no more pain, for the former things have passed away"* (Revelation 21:3b,4). A person is in Hell because he failed to receive Jesus Christ as personal Savior, the free gift of eternal life from God. A person is in Heaven because he received God's free gift, His Son Jesus Christ. *"We are confident [assured], yes, well pleased rather to be absent from the body and to be present with the Lord"* (II Corinthians 5:8).

Second, the Bible says **We are sinners**. *"For all have sinned and come short of the glory of God"* (Romans 3:23). We are sinners because Adam and Eve made a choice and it was the wrong one. They disobeyed God, therefore sin entered the human race. *"Therefore, just as through one man*

[Adam] sin entered, and death through sin, and thus death spread to all men, because all sinned" (Romans 5:12). *"For the wages of sin is death [physical and spiritual] but the gift of God is eternal life through Christ Jesus our Lord"* (Romans 6:23).

Third, the Bible says **Christ died for our sins**. Jesus was sinless and did not deserve death but He took our place on the Cross. *"For He [God the Father] made Him [Jesus] to be sin for us, who knew no sin, that we might be made the righteousness of God in Him"* (II Corinthians 5:21). *"Who Himself bore our sins in His own body on the tree [Cross], that we having died to sins, might live for righteousness, by whose stripes you were healed [spiritually]"* (I Peter 2:24). Jesus said, *"I am the Way, the Truth, and the Life, no man comes to the Father but by me"* (John 14:6). *"We were redeemed with the precious blood of Christ, as of a Lamb without blemish and without spot"* (I Peter 1:19).

Fourth, the Bible says **salvation is not of works**. *"For by grace you have been saved through faith, and that not of yourselves, it is a gift of God"* (Ephesians 2:8,9). A person can do all the good works in this life, but not one of them goes toward a person being saved. That's because salvation is free. A man in the New Testament asked, *"...What must*

I do to be saved? So they [Paul and Silas] said, Believe on the Lord Jesus Christ, and you will be saved, you and your household" (Acts 16:31).

Fifth, the Bible says **confess Christ.** *"If you confess with your mouth the Lord Jesus and believe in your heart that God has raised Him [Jesus] from the dead, you will be saved. For with the heart one believes unto righteousness and with the mouth confession is made unto salvation"* (Romans 10:9,10). *"For whoever calls on the name of the Lord shall be saved"* (Romans 10:13). In John 3:16 we're told that when we believe on Jesus, we shall not perish. Here in Romans 10:13 we're told that we will be saved. Saved from what? The term saved is speaking about being delivered from eternal torment and separation from God forever. In Revelation 20:11-15 we're told about books that were opened, *"And anyone not found written in the Book of Life was cast into the lake of fire"* (Revelation 20:15).

Would you like your name written in the Book of Life so that you might escape the lake of fire? If your answer is Yes, then right now, right where you are, you can pray and receive Jesus into your life. Pray something like this and mean it from your heart: "Dear Lord Jesus, I believe you are the Son of God and that you died for my sins, was buried and rose again. Forgive me of my sins. I ask you, Jesus, to be my Savior and forgive me of my sin. Thank you for the gift of eternal life and I pray this in Jesus name, Amen." The Bible says, *"...as many as received Him [Jesus], to them He gave the right [authority] to become children of God, to those who believe in His name"* (John 1:12).When you receive Christ into your life, you can literally say, I'm a child of God.

At the same time He gave you eternal life and you can trust God that right now Heaven is your eternal home. *"Truly, I say to you, he [that's you] who hears my word and believes in Him, has everlasting life [this is present tense; in other words, right now you have eternal life] and shall not come into condemnation [perishing in Hell], but has passed from death into life"* (John 4:24). By adoption you have been placed into God's family forever. Praise the Lord, Glory to His name!

Now repent [turn and go in the opposite direction] from your sins and turn to righteousness and serve God. *"For they themselves [people who received Christ as Savior] declare concerning us what manner of entry we had to you, turning from idols to serve the living and true God, And to wait for His Son from heaven, whom He raised [Jesus] from the dead, even Jesus who delivers us from the wrath to come"* (I Thessalonians 1:9,10).

Now that you are saved and have Heaven as your eternal home, along with those who are already Christians, it is vital that you grow in Christ. *"...but grow in the grace and knowledge of our Savior and Lord Jesus Christ"* (II Peter 3:18). Following are some things that will help you grow in your new life in Christ. I will use the letters of the word GROWTH to show you this.

G = Go to a Bible-believing church faithfully. Go to a church where the Bible is preached and taught from the pulpit, where people love the Lord Jesus. *"And let us consider one another in order to stir up love and good works, not forsaking the assembly of ourselves together..."* (Hebrews 10:24,25a)

R = Read the Bible daily. It is God speaking His truth to us. Read it, memorize it, study it so you know the truth. There was a group of people in a place called Berea, as told in Acts 17:11, and the Bible says *"These were more fair-minded than those in Thessalonica, in that they received the word with all readiness of mind, and* _searched the scriptures_ *[the Bible] daily to find out whether those things were so."*

O = Obey the Lord by being baptized (not for salvation, but as evidence of it). In Acts 2:41 we read that there were about 3000 people saved and on that same day they obeyed the Word of God by being baptized (by immersion). *"Then those who gladly received his word [were saved] were baptized..."* baptism is an outward display of an inward covenant.

W = Witness; that is, tell someone else that you received Christ as your personal Savior. We are told in the Bible to confess Jesus before men. Tell someone of your new life and it will clinch that decision in your mind and heart.

T = Take time to pray daily. In I Thessalonians 5:16 we're told to *"pray without ceasing,"* that is, always be in an attitude of prayer. *"Now it came to pass, as He [Jesus] was praying in a certain place, When he ceased, that one of His disciples said to Him, 'Lord, teach us to pray'..."* (Luke 11:1). God talks to us through His Word the Bible, and we talk to Him through prayer. Be faithful to pray daily.

H = Honor the Lord in every area of your life. *"And whatever you do in word or deed, do all in the name of the Lord Jesus, giving thanks to God the Father through Him...And whatever you do, do it heartily as to the Lord and not to men"* (Colossians 2:17,23). *"You are worthy, O Lord, To receive glory and honor and power..."* (Revelation 4:11a).

As a child of God, be faithful to live for Christ, presenting yourself to Him. *"I beseech [beg] you therefore, brethren, by the mercies of God, that you present your bodies a living sacrifice, holy, acceptable to God, which is your reasonable service. And do not be conformed to this world, but be transformed by the renewing of your mind, that you may prove what is that good and acceptable and perfect will of God"* (Romans 12:1,2).

I would encourage you as a Christian to read Ephesians 4:17-32 and Colossians 3:1-17. In both of these passages you will find the words 'old man' and 'new man'. The words 'old man' represent what you were, a sinner unsaved. The words 'new man' represent what you are now, a sinner saved by grace, a righteous person through Christ.

I hope and pray that this book of my experience through the deep, dark valley of depression has been a help to you. I hit bottom and survived. I climbed back to the mountaintop of victory and so can you. Yes, I do have limitations and I have learned to adapt to my situations. I've had to make changes in my life and in many areas I'm stronger than I was before. Just remember, *"...we are more than conquerors through Him who loved us"* (Romans 8:37b).

My hope is not a think-so but a know-so hope. The following lyrics describe my hope.

When We [I] See Christ

Verse 1:

Oft times the day seems long

Our trials hard to bear

We're tempted to complain

To murmur and despair

But Christ will soon appear

To catch His bride away

All tears forever over

In that eternal day

Chorus:

It will be worth it all

When we see Jesus

Life's trials will seem so small

When we see Christ

One glimpse of His dear face

All sorrow will erase

So bravely run the race

Till we see Christ

Verse 2:

Life's day will soon be o'er

All storms forever past

We'll cross the great divide

To glory safe at last

We'll share the joys of heav'n

A harp, a home, a crown

The tempter will be banished

We'll lay our burden down

Chorus:

It will be worth it all

When we see Jesus

Life's trials will seem so small

When we see Christ

One glimpse of His dear face

All sorrow will erase

So bravely run the race

Till we see Christ

Encouragement from the Bible, God's Word

The following verses are from Psalm 119

"This is my comfort in my affliction, For your word has given me life." (v.50)

Before I was afflicted I went astray, But now I keep your word." (v.67)

"It is good for me that I have been afflicted, That I might learn Your statutes." (v.71)

"I know, O Lord, that Your judgments are right, And that in faithfulness You have afflicted me."(v.75)

"Unless Your law had been my delight, I would have perished in my affliction." (v.92)

"I am afflicted very much, Revive me, O LORD, according to Your word." (v.107)

"Consider my affliction and deliver me, For I do not forget Your law." (v.153)

CPSIA information can be obtained at www.ICGtesting.com
Printed in the USA
BVOW021813150412

287734BV00001B/35/P